Living without a Mother

Marjerie Texas Lewis Romine

Living without a Mother

Marjerie Texas Lewis Romine

Parson's Porch
Books
Cleveland, TN

Parson's Porch Books

Copyright © 2011 by Marjerie Texas Lewis Romine

ISBN: Softcover   978-1-936912-36-0

This book was printed in the United States of America.

To order additional copies of this book, contact:

Parson's Porch Books
1-423-475-7308
www.parsonsporch.com

Cover Photo

Marjerie's Parents - 1915

Francis Ray Lewis

and

Ella Elizabeth "Null" Lewis

PREFACE

IN MY BOOK I WOULD LIKE TO enlighten today's young people of how my generation lived in the early 1900's. We had a happy Christian family life until the sudden loss of my mother in 1924 at the age of 29. Life changed for my father, sister, brother and I forever. I will share stories about people's lives through a child's eyes. Stories about my loving family that lived in West Virginia, and some adventures my siblings and I had while living in the city. Also, the wonderful times and events while living at our Grandmother Lewis's farm. Living with little or no modern conveniences and what people of that day had to do to survive without them. Read how our community, neighbors and the church were a major part of our lives. Love was, and still is the key to happiness and truth at all times.

The theme of my book is mostly about my life without a mother's guidance. The thoughts and wishes I had when I missed my mother. My father was 30 years old and did not remarry after my mother went to Heaven. I prayed to Jesus to help me to do my best with the responsibility I felt as the oldest girl. As you read my book remember each story has meaning, so enjoy! Live, laugh and love with God's blessing has been my motto for 93 years. I wish to thank everyone for their patience and understanding while enabling me to finish my book.

INTRODUCTION

My story begins at Rusk, West Virginia in 1915 before I was born. During that time families had lots of land and neighbors were few and far between. This resulted in limited choices for young adults to marry. In my father's situation he married my mother and his brother, married her sister. The great depression was a major factor for the shortage of jobs for men during a very discouraging era.

Goodyear Tire and Rubber was soliciting for workers to come to Akron, Ohio to be hired for jobs in their factory. So off they went, Dad, Francis Lewis and Mom, Ella Null Lewis for the good life, or so they thought. Two of the Lewis brothers had previously relocated. They helped to find apartments for my parents and my aunt and uncle who also came along. Dad rented a small apartment on the second floor of a big three story house. A couple on the first floor had an oil cooking stove against the stairway wall. I was told Dad cautioned them about the danger but they did not heed his warning.

Dad was hired at Goodyear. All the Lewis family were happily living close to one another. A year passed, then my brother Ronald was born in 1916. Soon after, Mom's sister arrived from West Virginia on the train to help with the new baby. She climbed the two flights of stairs carrying her heavy valise. Anxious to see her first nephew she rushed straight to the bedroom. He was awake and cooing and she thought he was the most adorable red headed baby.

Just a few minutes passed when someone on the first floor yelled, "FIRE'. Dad picked Mom up from her bed and started for the stairs.

Aunt Florie grabbed the baby and her valise then quickly followed them down the steps. The stairway ceiling was covered with tar paper and dropping pieces of hot flames.

Everyone escaped but Dad did get burns on his arms. Just a few homes had phones so by the time the fire department was even called it was too late. The fire trucks were pulled by horses in those days so it took a long time for them to get to a fire. That big old house burned to the ground within fifteen minutes. The next day Dad was searching through the ashes and some how found his pocket watch and mother's small golden chain watch. (I still have them in my old antique cedar chest.) They all moved in with family until they could find another place to live. Dad was very industrious and responsible so he soon found a little house at 783 E. Crosier St. There were only two houses on the block, ours and another one for rent. Finally another young couple moved in with their handicapped son. Mom was real anxious to meet them and did she ever get a surprise. It was her girlfriend from West Virginia, Jennie and husband Jim, what a happy reunion.

The four Lewis brother's all worked at Goodyear. Dallas said he didn't go to college to do manual labor so he quit.

Then he started his career at Prudential Insurance. Russell did not like the working conditions so Aunt Pearl and him moved back to the Lewis Homestead in West Virginia Guy and my Dad were the only brother's that stayed in Akron.

From what I was told the next two years past very quickly. During that time my brother became very spoiled by the family, but soon all that would change. Now the real story begins.

Chapter One
Living With Father And Mother

THE SECOND CHILD ARRIVED ON A COLD winter morning February 28, 1918 at 783 East Crosier Street Akron, Ohio. I'm telling this the way my Dad told it to me.

My little brother was sitting in his rocking chair in the corner of the small living room. He was whimpering softly as he heard his Mother cry out in the next room. He did not understand why he couldn't go to her. Dad was anxiously walking the floor and didn't seem to notice him. The neighbor woman had come to help the man in the bedroom Dad called the doctor. Mother gave a deep cry and my brother whimpered again real loud. Dad then looked around and realized he needed attention. He told me, he said to Ronald, "Poor little Ronald, I'll peel you an apple, you must be really hungry". He gave the apple to his son and he was satisfied for the time being. Then again Mother gave another sharp cry. The doctor was heard to say, "Fine, we have a baby girl." Then a baby cried loud and clear.

Dad gave a sigh of relief and fell into his chair. The neighbor woman came out of the bedroom with a blanket that moved. She handed the bundle to him and said ,"It's a sweet little girl." About that time the doctor came out and said "Everything will be all right." Dad thanked him and they shook hands before he left.

Dad said he looked down into the blanket and whispered "You are a cute little thing with bright red hair just like your Mother's."

He then turned to Ronald and said, "This is the new baby. Now you will not be able to sleep with your Mom any more." I was told my brother jumped up from his chair and slung his apple just as hard as his chubby arm could throw it. Dad caught the apple just in time to keep it from hitting his new sister in the head. Brother Ronald then let out a loud squall and screamed, "I want my Mommy." From the bedroom, Mother called out "I want to see my baby." Dad said he started walking quickly to her side with the new arrival but when he came through the door she said, " Not that one, I want my baby boy." That is the way it was the second child was never the baby. My brother took my place. Things changed later when another little red headed girl came along. He was forced to accept the new baby in the family.

Two years went by quickly. Something seemed to be very wrong at our house as my dad told this story to us later. Mommy was sick and the doctor was in the bedroom with her. Our neighbor Jennie, was there also. Daddy is walking the floor, Ronald and I are being very quiet. All at once they heard a baby cry. Jennie came out with a blanket and went into the kitchen. Soon she came back out of the bedroom and handed the blanket to daddy. He bent down and showed Ronald and I the prettiest big baby doll we had ever seen. She had red curly hair, brown eyes. "This is your baby sister", he said. Then he took her in to our mommy. She laughed and cried at the same time. "This is just what I wanted, another little girl."

She sure didn't turn out to be a baby doll, she cried a lot.

Ronald and I didn't pay much attention to her until she started walking. Then we accepted her as our sister.

I was always watching what my mother was doing during the day. She and I were at home alone all day. My brother Ronald was in school and baby sister, Francie was asleep in her crib so I had mother all to myself. Where ever she was I was there by her side watching every move. This day she was doing our washing in a big aluminum tub full of warm water and a washboard.

The tub had a place where the fels naphtha soap laid until she rubbed on a dirty spot so the clothes turned out spotless. My ornery brother tried real hard to see how dirty he could get his clothes. Daddy worked at Goodyear and that lampblack was real hard to wash out. Mother never complained about any of her housework, she always wanted everything to be clean. The clothes she hung outside on the clothesline looked so white and clean. In the afternoon when they were nice and dry she took them down and folded them carefully in a basket. She dampened the ones she was going to iron then placed them back in the basket. I watched her fold the sheets and put them in a dresser drawer without ironing them. Muslin sheets were very rough and uncomfortable to sleep on. Mother could not rest until she took the sheets out of the drawer and took the extra time to iron them.

Finally it was time for Ronald to come home from school. He was so spoiled and demanded his time with mother now. I was the second child so I always took advantage of anytime I spent with mother. I especially enjoyed that special time and will remember my day with little sister and as always staying close to my mother's side

Another time I was sitting in my little rocking chair quietly watching. Ronald was always causing a problem so mother whipped him with a razor strap and it barely touched the edge of his eye. He hollered and cried like he was killed. Mom put a cold cloth on his eye and held him in her lap. He would look at me and wink and then let out another squall. He wasn't hurt but wanted to be petted and worry mom. After awhile he climbed down and started playing. I never told on him because I knew even at that early age he just wanted special attention from our loving mother. I think he was a little jealous of us girls and needed extra time with our mother.

Our family was going to the Lewis farm in West Virginia by train. We were looking forward to visiting with Grandma Martha and Grandpa Charles. I can remember just a little bit of this trip because I was just four years old, little sister was only two and big brother was six. Photos of that trip helps me relay the story. Some of the details was told to me by my Father at a later date.

We had to be ready to meet the train in east Akron very early in the morning. My Mother rose early, around three a.m. to get the three of us dressed. Ronald was the biggest baby of all, she had to humor and pet him to get him ready to go. He mostly got his way with her. It was a long walk to the station in the wee hours of that dark morning, as I recall.

Father helped Mother on the train first, then she found seats for dad and the three of us. We could hear the train start, then the engineer blew the loud whistle. The train let out a big cloud of black coal dust and we were on our way. Of coarse Ronald wanted to get out of his seat and explore his new surrounding. The conductor told him to stay in his seat while the train was moving. My brother stuck his tongue out at him when he turned his back.

The first stop was Marietta, Oh. where we stayed one night. It seems to me they had a parrot in a cage in the foyer of the hotel. Little sister, Frances tried to talk to it, then it would coo and talk back to her. If I came close to the cage he would take a fluttering fit.

The next morning we caught a streetcar to Parkersburg, WV There we went to the train depot and headed towards Petroleum, West Virginia our last stop.

Grandpa Lewis was waiting at the depot in his two seated surrey. Dad loaded all the suitcases along with our family. Grandpa's team of beautiful thoroughbred horses started slowly then moved into a gliding trot all the way down the road about four miles. Then up the steep hill to the Lewis farm. Grandma was waiting on the big front porch with lots of hugs and kisses. The kitchen table was covered with good old country cooking, Grandma had prepared for us.

Grandpa wasn't very well, but later that evening he sat in the swing on the porch and sang to us children. "Oh my darlin, Nelly Gray, they have taken her away. I'll never see my darlin any more. They have taken her to Georgia to wear her life away a working in the cotton and corn. They have taken her to wear her life away and I'll never see my darlin any more." As a child I thought it was a very sad song but did not know the meaning at that time.

After getting acquainted with all the cats ,dogs and farm animals we were very tired and willingly went to bed. Francie and I got the soft feather tick to sleep on for our bed. Ronald had to share cousin Bob's bed. They were quite a team, what trouble one couldn't think of to get into the other one did. It was a great pleasure to be tucked to bed in a home made feather tick feeling loved. " Pleasant dreams", Grandma said after giving us all a big kiss goodnight.

The next morning I remember Grandma plucking her geese. She had a little stool to sit on while she held a goose between her legs then she plucked the down from it's breast. The goose would try to get away and honked like crazy. The other geese seemed to be upset waiting their turn. When Grandma had a bag full of feathers and down, she shooed the geese away. We kids knew better then to bother the geese. If we did, they would spread their wings and run after us. They could flog you with their wings and hurt you so we ran fast because we were really afraid.

There is a few events that I have never forgotten. One day sister Francie slipped through the yard gate and wandered down among the geese. Mom was frantic when she missed her especially when she saw the gate was wide open. The geese had just been fed clabber milk. When milk turned sour it was poured in a croft, a long wooden feeder, so more of them could eat at one time. Mom was calling out for my sister. She couldn't see her among the geese because she had a fluffy white dress on. Francie finally raised up from the feeder with both hands covered with clabber milk and it was all over her face. My Mom ran down the path and scattered the geese in all directions. She then carried little sister back to the porch, washed her face and hands and put clean clothes on her. All the older folks had quite a laugh over the incident. Grandma was real surprised the geese let her eat with them. She said, "Maybe they thought she was one of them."

We wondered down to the barn where all the new baby animals were. The lambs were so cute with their beautiful wooly coats. They didn't seem to be afraid of us. They came real close wanting to play scampering, jumping and showing off with their long tails waving.

At the buggy barn grandpa was repairing any thing he could find damaged. He kept the buggies in good shape because that was the only mode of transportation in the country. He took time out of his busy day to take us all to see the new hatched chicks. I thought he didn't feel good because he looked really tired to me. This day was very exciting for us city kids and we looked forward to tomorrow, another day of discoveries.

Next morning after breakfast we crossed the river in an old john boat to get to the Lewis homestead to visit my mother's sister, Aunt Pearl. Uncle Russell and her had a daughter named Rhoda. She was four the same age as I. We all went into the house. My cousin quickly went to the stairway and said, "Stay up there little red waggy til Paugy goes home". My brother nicknamed me Paugy. Mother didn't miss anything. She said to Aunt Pearl, "Are you hiding things from my kids?"

She replied, "It is just a little wagon and it can't be treated rough."" Mom brought it down stairs and gave it to Rhoda. She pulled it out to the porch. It was made of wood with wooden wheels and painted a beautiful red color. We always played real well together so she told me to get in first. She started pulling me in the wagon and it bounced off the porch. All four wheels collapsed. We both started crying. Her mother walked to the door and said "I knew this would happen." Ronald was watching, he said, "this is one accident that can't be blamed on me." Mom and Aunt Pearl started laughing to tears. I'm sure Mom was sorry about the broken wagon but it was just

19

one of the things that happens when kids play together. It wasn't too long before we were all playing happily again. Because I was so young I just remember a few memorable things about that vacation.

As a child we never had jell-o unless we had a deep snow. We had no electric lights or refrigeration, only an ice box. All our utilities were gas, even our lights. We always looked forward to a big snow so we could make frozen jell-o. Our mother would keep the jell-o on hand so we would always be prepared and never miss a time to make our favorite desert. At that time we could only purchase fresh fruit at the store apples, bananas and oranges. Also canned peaches to add to our jell-o. Mother keep English walnuts on hand as they were most important for jell-o to be crunchy and chewy. Us three kids were watching mother but all of a sudden Ronald threw in raisins before she could stop him. Mother made the jell-o in a large crock and put a tight lid on it.

In order for the jell-o to gel it had to be taken outside and be placed in the cold snow. I had to get dressed for the occasion by putting on my winter coat, toboggan and scarf. Then I put on my galoshes to keep my feet warm. We all went outside and mother dug a hole in the deep snow to place the crock. Then she pulled the snow up around it and covered it completely. Now it was my job to watch for any of the neighborhood dogs to keep them from getting close to our treasure. I had a big long stick as my weapon and woe to any dog, cat or kid that came close to it. I went in the house to warm up so I let Ronald take a turn. All he did was make snowballs then called to the kids watching to help him make a snowman. I soon came back outside and took over and told the kids to go home. I guarded that crock of my favorite dessert like it was a precious treasure. It was over an hour before mother came to check to see if it had gelled. I was glad to get back into the house because my feet were just about frozen. I watched through the window till daddy came home. Mother had supper and dad brought the big crock of jell-o inside. I got to take the lid off and everyone yelled "JELL-O." It was so delicious. We all had another dish before going to bed then it was all gone. That was a very happy memory of mine.

Everybody on the street was excited, kids and parents alike. The circus was coming to town! The circus traveled by train and big wagons were unloaded not too far away.

We lived close to the big lot where they set up for the performances for three straight days. We were all going, even our father.

All the kids lined up on the sidewalk to see the wagons parade before the big show. The Indians were driving the big wagons. Their horses were decorated with beaded harnesses and the Indians wore big feathers and head bands in lots of colors. Their outfits and moccasins were all made of leather. All the clowns faces were made up with paint, big noses, big red mouths and fancy costumes. The pretty ladies were in carriages and had decorated horses with bridals loaded with high pompoms standing straight up. I was especially frightened by the tigers, who looked so furious while pacing back and forth gnashing their teeth and growling with ugly sounds in their cages. They looked very hungry and never laid down.

When daddy came home from working at Goodyear, mommy had us ready to go to the circus. After supper we left the house and crossed down the street. We bought our tickets and started inside of the tent. Mommy was carrying two year old Francie. Ronald and I were holding onto daddy's hands. Somehow my hand slipped loose and I was pushed to the ground. Everyone was stepping on me and I began to scream. Daddy reached down to pick me up, but the crowd was so excited he couldn't reach me. Someone held the crowd back while daddy picked me up in his arms and carried me inside. We found mommy and she had saved seats for all of us. Everyone was pretty upset until the Ring Master said, "Welcome to the Greatest Show on Earth".

It was nothing like the circus we see today. Indians came out riding their horses all decorated with fancy saddles, yelling, shouting, and doing spectacular tricks. I thought they were fantastic. A large fence was erected in the arena and the tigers were released. The trainer snapped his whip and they took their places. I told mommy that I was scared of them, but Ronald said he wasn't. High in the tent the performers were flying and catching each other, swinging like monkey's. In another arena the elephants sat on their rumps and picked up their trainers with their trunks, and made loud trumpet sounds. At four years old I became very tired and I was ready to go home. The hard wooden benches were uncomfortable for all of us so we all headed back down the street to our house.

We certainly had no problems falling asleep that night. The next day Ronald said he wanted to go back again. Our parents said we had enough circus this year, but maybe next year we would go again.

Our neighbor Jennie and my mother decided to go Christmas shopping. Our only transportation was by city bus. Jennie had three kids and so did my mother. It was a job to get all of us a seat on the bus together.

The department stores had beautiful Christmas displays in their big windows outside. How exciting, a train running on a track blowing it's whistle, little elves making toys, and Santa in the background. It was hard to leave and go inside. I heard a clerk say "here comes Cox's army." I knew my mom didn't hear her because she would have been upset.

My mom was looking for yardage. She wanted material to make some Christmas clothes for us kids. She found what she was looking for, but then couldn't find her purse. It was gone! The clerk called the office and her purse had been turned into lost and found, but all the money was missing. That ruined our day so we could do nothing but take the bus back home.

When we arrived home I started to cry, as I didn't think Santa would bring me a little red rocking chair that I had asked him to bring me. Father was very disappointed as our Christmas would be sparse this year.

To my surprise Christmas morning guess what was under the tree for me? It was a little red rocking chair and a lovely baby doll with my name on it. I guess if you really want something bad enough and really believe, it just might happen. Thank God for loving parents and Santa Clause too!

Sometime in the summer of 1923 pretty exciting news sticks in my mind. The Lewis clan kept in touch with each other on a regular basis. We heard that Granddad Lewis had decided there was no reason why his youngest daughter shouldn't have a car. She was the only child still living at home and she was the apple of his eye I was told later.

He was hearing that some of the neighbors were talking about buying one of those fast machines called a car. He loved going to the fair every year but it sure took a long time to get there by horse and buggy he thought.

Early Saturday morning Grandma and daughter Lillie Ellen got ready to go to the local grocery store. They took ten dozen eggs at nineteen cents a dozen and five chickens to sell. They received a total of $5.72. They bought sugar and flour and had change left over. Ellen strolled outside to look over the cars for sale. She just knew she could drive, so she called her Mom outside to look one over. Mr. McFarland quickly followed them out. Like most car salesmen he told them how great it was and easy to drive. He motioned to them and said, "Come on, go for a ride and see how you like it."" They hopped right in and instantly loved it. Grandma replied, "You show Ellen how to drive then we'll take one." They bought that Model T Ford on the spot March15, 1923. A check for $25.00 was a down payment.

I guess it was a big surprise to Grand-dad when my Aunt Ellen drove up the hill in that new car while Grandma followed her in the horse and buggy. He was very pleased and proud of the Ford when he arrived at his destinations. All his friends greatly admired his pride and joy. He was especially excited about getting to the fair that year much faster then the year before.

Some of the first things I remember about my childhood still lingers in my memory vividly. The neighborhood kids all called our little house the barn house because the roof was shaped like a barn. They all liked to play in our big front yard. Most of the time we got our exercise playing tag, drop the hankie and hide and seek.

One of my fondest memories was of my Mother playing the old pump organ . I don't remember how she taught us the words to The Old Rugged Cross and In The Garden but I have never forgotten them. My brother, Ronald stood up straight and tall and sang with all his might just to impress Mom. I stood on the other side of her and sang melody while she sang alto very softly. Little sister, Frances listened to us while playing with her toys. I was 4 or close to 5 years old at that time.

When I turned five I started to kindergarten. It was my first day to go to school . I was a little frightened. Mother took me and of course went in to meet the teacher. She explained that I was left handed . The teacher said she would fix that. When Mother left she said for me to pick up the pencil . I picked it up with my left hand and whammo, she hit my knuckles with her ruler. I sure didn't know what I had done wrong. She frowned at me and said to always use your right hand when writing. I looked at her and said, "My Dad uses his left hand ." She then replied , "Your daddy is not your teacher I am, now put the pencil in your right hand." I tried to hold it as she said but it dropped to the floor. She raised her ruler again. She then wrote A on the chalk board and we were supposed to copy it.

I was so relieved. I quickly picked up my pencil. Then I slowly drew a straight line then tried to fasten another line to it and crossed it with another line. The teacher came by and thought I did a good job. To please my teacher I overcame writing left handed. I caught on quickly and wanted to learn. Later in the year I thought she was a good teacher and was real proud of me.

I'll never forget the first papers I brought home for Mom and Dad to see. I still remember that day as if it was yesterday. When I walked in Dad was giving Mommy a great big hug and kiss. When I proudly handed them my school papers they both bent over and laughed loudly. I said, "I could have done so much better but I was so nervous." They just laughed more. As I went over to my security chair and started rocking, it was my precious hiding place and my comfort. They stopped and told me my writing was just beautiful. I always wondered why my school papers caused them to laugh so hard.

I was looking out the window feeling sorry for myself. It was cold and dreary outside and I felt cold and dreary inside. I remember this event in my life very vividly. It was December of 1923. Christmas season had finally arrived. To a five year old it has been a long time coming. Now it was all for nothing. Mother was ill and we wouldn't be able to take our special Christmas stroll. Each year we went downtown to see the exciting window displays in the big stores. I wanted in the worst way to go and tears were in my eyes.

Just then someone knocked on the door. It was our new neighbor, Mrs. Doy. She had stopped to inquire of Mother's health. I greeted her with a feeble hello and a tear stained face.

"Now what is wrong with little Marjie?" she asked? "I want to see the Christmas windows downtown," I replied "but Mother is ill and can''t take me this year." "What a coincidence, I am on my way downtown and would be happy to take you, that is if you promise to hold my hand," Mrs. Doy exclaimed.

My face brightened. "Please Mamma, I will never let go of her hand, I promise." Mother wanted me to be happy so she gave her permission. We were soon ready to leave.

"You have forgotten something very important," Mother said softly. "Let us bow our heads for prayer. Dear Heavenly Father, watch over us and keep us in thy tender care. Bring my little girl back home safely, in Jesus name, Amen."

As I walked down the drive I turned and saw Mother waving. Concern showed on her face and she seemed to foresee something unpleasant for me. In the excitement, Mother was soon forgotten. We stepped off the bus into a fantasy land of gold and silver tinsel strung everywhere. Red and green wreathes on lamp posts, bright blinking lights all around. Forgetting my promise, I broke loose from Mrs. Doy's hand and pushed through the crowd to the window. It was all and more than I had ever dreamed. I pressed my nose tightly against the glass.

Santa was waving to me; his small helpers were sawing, hammering and painting toys all moving in rhythm. Reindeer were prancing; a toy train was running around on a track, movement was everywhere. All this seemed to hypnotize me.

In the distance I heard Mrs. Doy say, "Come Marjie, we must go now, I have some shopping to do." I started to go to her but stopped, I stood there in a daze, I couldn't move, time slipped away.

When I looked around, most of the people were gone. Where was Mrs. Doy? Had she gone home without me? I was terrified. What must I do?

Mother had told me to find a policeman if I ever got lost. I looked around and right there on the corner he stood, just as if he had been waiting for me. Quickly I walked over to him and tugged at his sleeve. Startled he looked down.

"Well hello there little girl, is there something wrong?" He asked. My voice cracked and big tears started to roll down my cheeks, "I'm lost,"" was all I could say. "Now, now, don't cry. Everything will be all right. Do you know your address" he asked? I shook my head yes but couldn't answer. At that very moment, a lady walked over and said, "I know this little girl, her mother is a friend of mine." ""Oh, Mrs. Shaffer, I'm so glad you found me," I cried.

On the bus I snuggled up close to her. I had time to think, if I hadn't broken my promise, none of this would have happened. It was my fault. I wondered if Mother knew I was lost? She would be very unhappy. My question would soon be answered.

As I opened the kitchen door, I saw my mother kneeling at a chair her head in her hands. She was praying, "Dear Heavenly Father, please bring my little one back home safely.""

I ran over to her and put my arms around her neck and kissed her. "Momma, momma, please don''t cry. Jesus answered your prayer and kept me safe. He even sent Mrs. Shaffer to find me."

Mother took me in her arms an in a trembling voice said, "Thank God for answered prayer and thank God for Mrs. Shaffer."

It was February and too cold for me to walk to school. I was happy because my mom was making beautiful home made valentines. She could make them look like they came straight from heaven because they looked like angels. I watched as she made each one more beautiful then the last.

Finally she handed me one and said," Take this over next door to Jennie my best friend."" I just stood for awhile and gazed at it and thought it was too beautiful to give away. I felt real bad to be so selfish when mom said, "Go ahead now you know Jennie hardly ever gets pretty things. Don't you want her to have something pretty and you will be the one to bring it to her''? I thought what if someone would feel this way about me. Mom said, "Come back quickly and see what I have for you".

I hurried over to Jennie's calling for her to open the door to see what my mom had made especially for her. She looked at the valentine and I saw tears in her eyes. She said, ""thank your mom for me". I rushed home in that cold winter air wondering why Jennie had cried. I thought maybe that's what friends do when they love each other.

I found out later that my mom and Jennie where special friends in West Virginia long ago when they where young, that made a difference.

When I arrived back home mom handed me a valentine. She had drawn a little red headed girl that looked just like me holding a valentine. I didn't know she could draw. It was lovely, just right for a five year old girl. It made me feel so good and very much loved. She made valentines for all the family each one very special.

Jennie was my mom"s special friend. One good friend can be more precious then a diamond you will ever get to wear. They can comfort you, cry with you when your lonely, laugh with you when you are happy and love you unconditionally.

It was a cool spring that year but hot summer days had finally arrived. What a wonderful time we were going to have at the Lewis family picnic. We all looked forward to the trip to Springfield Lake Park a short ways out of Akron. It was convenient for our whole family to meet for our time together. The ladies carried picnic baskets filled with good old fashion favorite dishes prepared by great cooks. We all then boarded the streetcar taking us straight to the park.

Trouble started real soon as usual, between my brother Ronald and our cousin Bob. Dad separated them until we arrived. Every one of us kids lined up and went from one uncle to another collecting change for all the rides.

Now you understand why we loved to go, it was also an amusement park along with the picnic grounds.

Our lunch was spread out on a long picnic table with benches along the sides. What a delicious meal and a happy time we all had .We were eating like little pigs when Aunt Isabelle yelled out, " Save some room for watermelon later"!

All of us kids rode the rides in the park while the adults caught up on the family news. That hot summer day in 1924 was such a special time for our family to be together. We became better acquainted with the many cousins that we didn't get to see very often. The red ripe watermelon was the big treat of that wonderful picnic.

At the end of the day we were all tired and ready to board the streetcar heading home. The little ones were cranky so I'm sure their Mother's were glad the day was ending.

As we were bidding our goodbye's I heard someone say, " It has been a good day, tomorrow we will see each other at church, God has been so good to all of us thank you Lord."

We had so many good times in our large Lewis family. There were 4 brothers and their wives, three sisters and their husbands and 7 children. We really loved one another and looked out for each other.

We were planning to all meet at Christmas again but that did not work out .That Christmas our lives would change forever .

With the hot weather which started around the time of our family picnic, my long straight hair was even more troublesome. Each night mother had to roll my hair in rags which was quite a lot of work for her. My hair would not stay curled no matter what she tried.

It was early morning and mother was just now able to take the time to comb my hair. A knock at the door and who was there but my Uncle Harry. "What's going on here," he asked? I began to whimper as mother started combing my hair. My uncle spoke up to mother saying, "For heaven's sake Ellie, how long are you going to torture this child by keeping her hair long it tangles and twists making it so hard to comb"? Of course I squirmed and let out another little moan. My mom looked at me and said, "does it really hurt that bad?" "Yes mommy, it hurts bad every time you comb it out."

"I think she would look great with bobbed hair and what a lot of time and work it would save you too," said uncle.

Mother said, "Her father would have a fit if her hair was cut, just like the time I wanted to get my hair cut and he just looked at me and laughed jokingly saying, I don"t believe you will." One of my fondest memories was my mother"s very beautiful long copper red hair, down to her waist and it would shine in the sun like precious diamonds. No wonder Dad did not want her to get it cut.

My uncle said, ""Well maybe it's time for a change in hair styles and Marjerie can be the first, and he'll just have to get used to it." Mother smiled and said, "Well, you are right he always has had his own way. Today maybe we can make him change his mind for once. There isn't a beauty shop close by here, and I cannot take her very far."

My uncle smiled and gladly offered to take me. Well, to make a long story short, mother finally gave in without asking dad and handed my uncle the money for my hair cut. He did not tell mother he was taking me to a barber shop just around the corner, not a beauty shop. The barber helped me climb up into the big men's leather chair. He wrapped a white clothe around my neck and he began to comb my hair. I looked all around and I was way up high in the air. There was nothing in the room but two other big chairs, a shelf with drawers and a lot of mirrors. He asked if he could braid some of my long hair and give it to me for a keepsake. What a good idea I thought. He plaited my hair into a braid, cut it, and laid it on the counter. I asked Uncle Harry if he would hold my hand and then he pretended he was keeping me from falling. As the scissors started cutting the hair that was left, I wondered if I really wanted to part with it? But I remembered what mother had told me, bobbed hair was latest fashion and I would be right in style. He turned me around and I looked in the mirror and liked what I saw, especially the bangs. Uncle Harry said he did too! As the barber took the clothe from around my neck he turned the chair so I could see myself front and back. I was so excited I couldn't believe it was me. I looked so different. I said, "It looks wonderful and I am sure my mother will like it but my father may not." The soft brush on my neck felt good as he finished. I was lifted down from the big chair and walked around looking at my new hair style in the mirrors. I asked for my braid to take home to my father, the barber had tied a ribbon on it and boy was it pretty.

Uncle Harry paid the barber for my haircut. Before leaving I opened my hand holding a dime and said to the him, "I would like to give you a tip for being so nice. My mother gave it to me to buy an ice cream cone, but now you can buy yourself one."" He smiled and said, "this is one of the most special tips I have ever received, thank you very much."

My uncle held my hand all the way home and I think I skipped every step. Little sister Francie was waiting at the kitchen door when we arrived. She clapped her hands and said, "pretty, pretty Paughy." Remember, that was the nick name given to me by my brother as he couldn't say Marjerie. He was standing there with his arms crossed on his chest and said, "I reckon it will have to do, but wait till dad gets home." Just about that time he saw dad coming home from work and he started to go out the door. Mother grabbed him by his shirt and jerked him back inside and said, "You sit down there and don't open your mouth." He looked really disappointed. I ran and hid behind my uncle. Dad looked all around and saw the other kids and said, "Where is Marjie"? I jumped out into the room and danced around for him to see my hair. He exploded and said,

"What happened to your hair"? I explained, Uncle Harry took me to get it cut and I really like it. Dad sat there for a while and finally said, "I do too." After that my hair was never mentioned except by my brother who said, " I can always pull your short hair if I want to just like I did your long red hair," but he never did again.

Way back in 1924, what was the most exciting thing that could happen in a kid's life? Of course, the circus coming to town! Last year we were unable to go to the circus but this year it would be a different story. I was six years old and I could remember a lot more now then when we went the first time. We still lived on East Crosier St. in Akron, Ohio. The circus would be unloaded from the train about a mile down the street. At that time the railroad was the most important form of transportation for most business and for long distance travel for the general public. Great news came that the parade would be coming up our street just like before. As usual all the neighborhood lined the sidewalk to watch the big event.

Our Mom didn't feel too well so her sister, Aunt Mary was with us to help supervise our behavior. I recall the big wagons with their wheels all decorated. Indians drove the wagons. They were dressed in leather, just like I remembered. Colored feathers in their hair, waving their bows and arrows as if they were trying to scare us. Clowns with painted big eyes and red noses and mouths. Elephants clomped with huge heavy feet being led by their trainers. Music was playing loudly, we all looked and there was a strange looking man playing his small music box while his trained monkey danced. All the kids were delighted to see this for the first time. He was called an organ grinder.

We begged our Mom to take us to the circus this year as we missed going last year. She agreed after talking to Dad. It seemed a long time to wait until tomorrow, but we did.

It was a short distance from our home so we were the first group there. Mom took care of four year old Francie and I. Our aunt took Ronald's arm.

He was only eight but big and strong and very excited so she had her hands full. Almost immediately I was in a trance watching the three rings full of entertainment. The ponies were marching in line, Indians riding and racing each other, whooping and showing off their weapons. The huge elephants pretending to step on their trainer scared me. Then they picked him up with their trunk and took him for a ride. Looking way up high in the air, pretty girls were swinging on ropes then suddenly men would catch them. How I wished I could do that some day. Little sister was laughing and clapping her hands, she was so delighted. Again the ugly little man was marching around playing his loud music while his energetic monkey danced. That monkey jumped up and wound the music box himself, that was unbelievable to me at the time. Tigers were let out of their cages. The trainer snapped his whip and they quickly took their places. He made them jump through hoops of fire and they did not like that. I was getting tired of sitting on those old, hard, wooden benches like the last time. Mom said it was time to go because Dad would be home from work soon for his supper. It was a struggle to get my brother ready to leave. Aunt Mary meant business though, when she twisted his ear and didn't let go.

It was nice to be safely home again from the noise and excitement. What a time we had telling our Dad about the huge three ring circus. That night I screamed in my sleep. I dreamed I was on a very high ferries wheel and could see the whole circus at one time. That nightmare was very scary and I woke up with a sigh of relief. I never told my Mom about my dream, but was so glad the circus would not come to town for at least another year.

Mom and Dad were sitting at the kitchen table and I knew by the look on their face they were going to talk seriously. I wanted to hear what they were going to say so I sat real still and listened quietly.

Finally Dad said, "Ellie don't you think we should start looking for a car? All the guys at the shop at Goodyear are bragging on their Model T. How much money do we have saved? I want to drive to WV so Ma won't have to pick us up at the train depot in her buggy." Mom said, "I counted it up and we have about four hundred dollars." "Well, that is not enough, the car is about five hundred dollars so we will have to cut down on our bills and save more" he replied.

It was July when Daddy came to Mom again and gave her his paycheck. She looked at it and said: "I think we can make it in a couple more weeks." "Fine , he said "why don't you and I go look at the model Ts" ? Jennie our next door neighbor looked after my sister and I. They took my brother Ronald because he could walk with them. Now everything was arranged. Off they went looking for a new car. All of them were Motel T's and everyone of them black. When they returned Daddy said we would get a car real soon.

We were really excited as our Uncle Dallas took us shopping in his new car and we loved it. Now we would have one of our own. It was a very happy time in our lives.

As Dad had promised, he bought a Model T and here he came proudly driving up our driveway. We all immediately climbed in, Mom in the front seat and us three kids in the back. All the way down the street we waved at all the kids along the sidewalk. They ran along side the car as we could only drive about 10 miles an hour.

We went driving every evening so Dad could learn to drive safe on our future trip to Grandma's in West Virginia.

I remember one time a boy ran out in the street after his ball and Dad had to step on the brakes real hard. It jerked all of us kids out of our seats and threw us around in the car. Mother called the boy over to her side of the car and told him to never run out in front of a car again. She was really upset.

Dad told Mom we should be ready to go to Wst Virginia to visit grandma Lewis this next weekend. We did not suspect this would be the last trip to the farm as a whole family. Mother was so proud of our 1924 Model T Ford. We three kids couldn't wait to get outside to spread the news to all our neighborhood friends. They wanted to know if our dad was going to drive our new car all that way. Ronald spoke up and bragged, ""You sure don't think we're going to walk do you?"

All during the week Mom was so busy cleaning, washing clothes, packing two suitcases and picking up little gifts to take to the family. She was worn out by the time we were ready to go. My Mom was the first one up about 5 am to pack a nice lunch for us to eat on the long trip. We hoped to get to Grandma's by supper time. Well, we were anxious to get started so we quickly piled in the back seat half asleep. Then Mom laid a quilt over our laps to keep us warm. Dad wasn't the best driver in town because back then you didn't need a drivers license you just learned to drive on your own. After cranking and cranking the car finally started and we were on our way straight down old route 21 heading south to West Virginia.

First thing Ronald wanted to do was eat as usual. Mother kept the lunch basket up front with her where she knew it would be safe. The gas stations were few and far between. We called them filling stations at that time. Dad had to stop pretty often because antifreeze was not invented yet. The car did not take much gas but sure needed a lot of water. We were all hungry but dad kept driving until Mom insisted he pull over for lunch about noon. We all jumped out, then under a barbed wire fence we crawled to reach a big shade tree. Mom laid a nice white sheet down and we had a picnic lunch that tasted like a feast made by an angel. On our way again, not stopping till dusk finally we arrived at our grandparents farm. We were too late for supper. Just in time for a big kiss from Grandma then off to bed to dream about tomorrow.

Our families 1924 vacation in West Virginia was about to begin. The next morning was very exciting for us. We always had a good time at the Lewis farm. There was a lot of space to run and play and many new things to see and learn. We were older now and could appreciate and understand more about the farm and the animals. Our cousin Bob who lived there was the same age as brother Ronald. They were stuck like glue and that spelled trouble. Francie and I played together and stayed close in the big yard.

Grandfather Lewis had passed away and we missed him very much. There was a great void in the family. We saw Grandmother wipe away tears with her apron and knew she really missed him also. As children we understood more then our parents realized. Our Dad's mom always taught us to be polite, shake hands with adults and say thank you. Moms family was especially affectionate so we loved to visit them too.

The next day Father drove Mother over to stay with her parents just a short distance down the windy road. Mother stayed with her family most of the time, they all loved her. In my eyes she seemed to be the favorite member of that family. There were 2 sisters Grace and Mary and their brother Andrew still living at the home place. Our aunts and uncle spoiled us while we stayed at their farm and we sure loved that.

Our uncle Russell Lewis had passed away from a bad accident. He was married to my Mother's sister Pearl. Their daughters Rhoda and Monelle was adopted by our grandparents and lived at the Null farm. Grandma had her hands full. The girls were well taken care of and we loved playing with them because they were about our age.

While we were there all of us attended Racy Baptist church where Grandma taught Sunday school. It was quite crowded with all of us in one house. We were all very happy being together with much harmony because happy people make happy families.

Grandma Null had a small store in front of the house close to the road. We loved looking at all the wonderful merchandise. This kept her pretty busy. Customers came from miles around to buy goods at her Gillispie, West Virginia store. People in the country had no way to travel very far and there was no other store close by. She would generously trade her goods for farm produce if they had no money. The merchandise consisted of mostly yard goods, kitchen utensils, clothing, shoes, towels, sheets and a few groceries, just the necessities. Our special treat was the stick candy she always had behind the counter. In the back she had a millinery shop. She designed beautiful hats for summer and winter wear. All of the ladies were thrilled to be able to get such lovely fashion locally. Her talent and creativity was widely known. As I recall on one occasion a big strong man stomped into the store. He was wearing oversized shoes that made a lot of noise. My Grandma said, "John why do you buy such big shoes? Let me help you with a pair that will fit your feet.'" They will feel better and you will walk a lot quieter. He said ,"'Well I thought I could get more shoe for my money but I guess your right I will try on a pair." She measured his feet and then fitted him with the right size. When he got up and walked he said, "They sure do feel good I will take them." She was a very clever and wise salesperson.

Grandfather Null was a very large man. He would take us kids up the hill to the sheep barn and show us all the newborn lambs with their long tails. They ran and played while the mother sheep closely watched them. Then he took us to the great big barn where he milked the cows. The many cats that lived in the barn followed him all around until he filled their milk bowls morning and night. The cows had to be milked twice a day. He was such a nice Grandpa and loved all of his grandchildren a lot and we knew it.

The farms were a wonderful place for an education because we learned how our ancestors lived and survived in older times. They raised most of their food in the garden and canned it for the winter months. An abundance of fruit trees provided for delicious pies for dessert on those cold winter days. There was no machinery to help with the labor at that time. Horses pulled plows so grain and corn were planted by hand.

They built their own homes, barns and out building that they needed. The first machinery I remember was the tractor. It was much faster and much easier on the farmers. They raised large families and every child had a chore to do each day. Every Sunday they went to Church as a family. It was a healthy, happy time to be alive. How proud we all should be of our ancestors.

When it was time to start back to Akron we had to say our goodbyes. First we kissed our Grandmother Lewis and said we would be back soon we hoped. Over to the other grandparents we drove down that windy road for the last time that summer. Grandma Null always packed our car with new sheets, towels and clothes for us kids.

She loved to hug and kiss us especially our Mother. It always made us feel loved very much.

We climbed in our car and Dad drove down that country road headed north back to Ohio. We arrived home to our neighborhood and friends to live the city life again. Ronald had big stories to tell his friends about our wonderful vacation in the country. That was the last trip to West Virginia our Mother took in our Model T car.

40

After returning home to Akron from our West Virginia vacation, Mom began having another episode of ill health. This went on for a short time, and then her health seemed to recover.

Then in the first part of December 1924 Mom became very ill and soon required a few days at the hospital in Akron. This would make her second time she needed care. I over heard some of the adults talking quietly saying that this time it could be serious. But Mother surprised us all.

We were so excited, Mother was coming home from the hospital. Father moved her bed into the living room where she could watch what we kids were doing. We were close by in case she needed us. It was still cold weather and the coal heater was in the living room where Ronald could help Mother keep the fire going. He was anxious to help because he loved our Mother very much and wanted her to get better. It was so nice to have our Mother back home.

My Aunt Maude and cousin Dorothy came over about everyday or so to cook our evening meals. This was a great help to Mom and Dad and us kids loved playing with our cousin.

Our kitchen and living room floors were linoleum because they were easier to mop and keep clean.

Mother looked into the kitchen and saw the floor was dirty with foot prints. She just couldn't stand for anything to be dirty. I was sitting quietly in my little rocking chair watching. Mother climbed out of bed to get her mop and bucket ,then filled it with soap and warm water. She mopped the floor very slowly, resting many times. When she finally finished she put the mop and bucket away. It wasn't very long until father came home from work.

He said, "This floor looks really clean, who mopped it for you?" I looked at Mother ,I knew what she meant when she looked at me and put her finger over her mouth. Mother answered, "Jennie came over and mopped it for me." Father told her it was sure nice of Jennie to do that.

Mother did not feel good that night as she had over worked herself. The next morning she whispered to me, "Don't tell Daddy about me mopping the floor because he wouldn't approve." I whispered back, "Mommy I will never tell, " and I never did.

A few weeks later I will never forget that snowy, windy day December 23, 1924. It was the last day I saw my Mother alive.

We were standing in the kitchen together. She looked all around as I heard her say, "If I don't come back they can't say my house was dirty." She had been scrubbing and cleaning all week. Washing windows, mopping floors, and cooking extra food for us for while she would be gone.

I looked up at her with tearful eyes. My mother looked beautiful to me with her fiery red hair showing from under her hat. She wore a long coat that almost touched her shoes. A tiny blue purse was on her shoulder and she carried a small valise that held her clothing. She leaned down and kissed me goodbye, and then walked out the back door.

Waiting in the 1924 Model T Ford was dad. My Aunt Maude and next door neighbor Jim Burghy were also going. They were taking Mother to Cleveland Lakeside Hospital. It was zero weather that holiday season in Ohio. It was a very long cold trip in an open car from our home in Akron.

That Christmas eve we three kids were all excited about Santa Claus coming during the night to bring our presents. Uncle Andrew from West Virginia, my mother's brother, was staying with us until he found a job. He was a lot of fun and always helped our mother cook and clean house. My uncle and Dad were whispering a lot that evening, we were too. We didn't know what might happen because our mommy was in the hospital. Maybe Santa would not come this Christmas eve.

It was dark and little four year old sister Francie was getting sleepy so daddy decided it was time for us to go to bed. Of course, Ronald objected as he was too nosey to sleep, but we were put to bed anyway. Ronald wouldn't sleep nor would he let Francie and I sleep. There was a lot of noise going on downstairs and he wanted to hear it all. He pulled us out of bed and took us to the stairway. Uncle Andrew was whistling and moving about and daddy was busy too. Ronald whispered to Francie and I, "There is no Santa Claus that's just Dad and Uncle Andrew putting out our presents, there is no Santa Claus"! Well, Francie began to cry so he grabbed her and carried her back upstairs to bed. All three of us finally went to sleep

We were up early Christmas morning and to our surprise Santa did come. Brother had a sled and an erector set. We girls unwrapped each a doll. I had a doll bed, and Francie a doll buggy. We were very happy but we missed our Mother. Our tree wasn't very pretty, dad had decorated it, but I was sure mom would have done a better job. I realized later in my life that before she left for the hospital she made sure her children would have a wonderful Christmas Day without her.

Later in the day I asked daddy, "Daddy where has mommy gone, where can she be, why didn't she come home and trim our Christmas tree? Big brother looks a fright, baby sister cries all night. I am sad and frightened too. Daddy, daddy what about you""?

Tears started streaming down his face, he placed me in his lap with a big embrace, and said, "You look so much like your mommy with her bright red hair. Don't be sad, mommy will be home soon with her happy cheer". I have always wondered about that Christmas day in 1924.I think my dad was sure his beloved wife would return to her loved ones. We would all then be one big happy family again.

A few days later I remember a very young boy delivering a telegram to our house. He looked so cold and sad standing on our front porch. The telegram was from the hospital saying, "COME QUICKLY! WIFE IS SERIOUS!"

Dad immediately started getting ready to leave. If I remember right, he heated bricks to take in the car for foot warmers. It would be a long cold trip to Cleveland. Aunt Maude and Jim Burghy would again travel with him.

I was told on the way the radiator froze up, and Dad covered it with his overcoat but it still took precious time before it thawed out enough to start again.

In the meantime at home another telegram was delivered from the hospital, this time is read, URGENT COME AT ONCE! When they finally arrived at the hospital the doctor was waiting to talk to them. Sadly he told them mother had died just twenty minutes before they arrived. What a great disappointment. Some time later the attending nurse told them that mother had died calling for her children.

When dad came back home on December 31,1924 he told us mother wouldn't be coming home from the hospital. At ages, four, six and eight we really didn't understand.

In Akron there was a small service for her many friends and neighbors. Mother was then taken to West Virginia and shown at her families home. She was laid to rest in the Mason Cemetery, not far from where she was born 29 years earlier. She was dearly loved by all her family and friends. Mother was a Christian so I was sure I would see her once more when I got to heaven. If she had lived I know I would have become a nurse, Francie a secretary and Ronald would have been much happier. He loved her so much and I know she would have encouraged him to do whatever he wanted to do with his life.

After awhile we returned home to Akron. My mothers sister Mary came back with us and stayed for some time. She spoiled Francie and gave her a lot of attention. She was a very sweet child.

I never knew how lonesome my father must have been losing Ella, his wife at such a young age. In the future years of my childhood I would find out what a difference a mother makes in a family.

Chapter Two
Living with Father alone

I COULDN'T GET THE TRIP FROM WEST VIRGINIA to Ohio out of my mind. Many times during my childhood I would lay awake trying to remember every detail of that sad ride home. I could vividly recall my Father packing the Model T Ford for our journey. It was January 8th, 1925 a very early, cold, snowy morning. The car had to be cranked then finally it started. The icing glass curtains were installed to keep out some of the cold. We were all bundled up with quilts. Francie was in the front seat on Aunt Mary's lap all wrapped up. Ronald and I were in the back warm as toast. The roads were slippery so Father drove slowly. Soon it was time to stop for gas and eat our lunch. The station manager was kind and invited us to eat inside. At that time there was no restaurants or McDonalds and very few gas stations. It was a long trip and it was dark when we arrived in Akron. Dad lit his lantern so we could get to the house safely. He unloaded a few of the necessary supplies while our Uncle Andrew greeted us with milk and donuts. My Father quickly went to the basement and started a fire to warm our old house. We three kids were quickly hustled off to bed. Even as tired as I was I remember being so disappointed my Mother was not there to tuck us into bed.

My life had changed, now it would be living with father alone. I would be 7 years old in 6 weeks. At that age of course, I didn't realize how my life's journey would be different living without a Mother then other children's.

The next morning my brother and I did not fully understand the situation without our Mother being there. Little sister was too young to know there was any difference. We seemed to adjust to our Aunt Mary staying with us. She was so good to us almost like our Mother. Our Father appreciated her help and the care she gave us. If not for her kindness he could not have kept his job at Goodyear as a carpenter. He worked every day except Sunday. Sometimes we were a problem for her but she was very patient and loving. She tickled Ronald's back at night till he fell off to sleep. She was especially fond of baby sister. Rocking her and singing to me was a special time in my life. We loved her hugging and kissing us and making over us when we needed it most.

While our Aunt was staying with us several interesting events happened. One of them is when Dad and his brother, who lived next door decided to have city water installed at the same time. What a great improvement that would be. They were hard at work digging a four feet deep ditch from the street to the houses so the water line would not freeze in the winter. From the front porch Aunt Mary, Francie, and I were watching them work, but where was my brother? We would find out later! When dinner was ready Dad said it would have to wait while they cleaned up before they could eat. While we waited on the porch we spied Ronald sitting at the table eating nearly all the fried chicken. Aunt Mary was really angry! She ordered him to leave the table and get out on the front porch. Did it bother him? No way, he was full of chicken. When the men finally came in to eat Dad asked, "Where is the chicken?" I didn't dare say a word. Aunt Mary spoke up and said, "Ronald got hungry and couldn't wait, so he helped himself and filled up on chicken."" Dad just stared at him and shook his head. I know he was disappointed because he wanted for his brother Guy to have a good meal after all that hard work. From then on it was live and learn when it came to feeding Ronald. We were all delighted when the plumbing and running water was installed. What a joy getting a drink from the spigot. Taking a nice warm bath in a big, white, clean tub and relaxing. Going to an inside toilet and not being afraid after dark of falling in a hole rushing to the outside privy. It was rare for a family to gain this improvement during my childhood. Good clean water can never be measured but for the joy and comfort we were blessed to have in those days.

Another special time was when we saw a big moving van coming up the street while we were playing in our yard. It was going real slow so we guessed a new family was moving to our neighborhood. How excited we were to think we might have more playmates. My nosey brother and I took off at a trot to watch the men unload the huge van. We saw them carry into the house bunk beds, boy's furniture, and a big box with basketballs, footballs, and lots of other boy's toys. Soon the new family drove up in an old Dodge touring car. Out jumped two boys. One was about nine and the other about twelve. Their Dad was carrying a beautiful little girl to the house as their Mom followed. Ronald was not bashful when he asked the youngest boy, "What's your name and how old are you?" He replied smiling, ""My name is Kelly and I am nine." My brother said to him, "I'm Ronald and I am also nine. This is my sister Marj and she is seven. We live nearby and we would like to show you around. That is, if it is ok with your folks." Kelly said, "I have to go inside now but I will ask. I will see you soon, good bye for now." We skipped home excited about our new friend.

We were up early the next morning and crossed the street into a big open field. We walked real slow gazing at the ground for mice nests. Ronald yelled, "Come quick and see the baby mice." The mother was gone so he picked up a pink, squirmy little bit of an animal and handed it to me. He then picked up the last three and we headed home on the run. Kelly was on the sidewalk watching. He asked, "What do you two have there?" "Just a nest of four baby mice, answered my brother." "What are you going to do with them?" Kelly asked. "I don't know, maybe kill them," brother said sheepishly. Kelly said, "I don't think you should do that. I bet their mother is looking for them right now. Why don't we go see?"" Ronald hesitated then said, "OK, maybe we can catch the mother too." Of course that is not what our friend wanted to hear. I'm sure he was hoping we would leave the babies back at their nest. Off we went looking for that tiny nest. It was hard to find among all the weeds but there it was! The mother was back in the nest. We scared her and of course she quickly ran away. We coaxed Ronald to put the baby mice back gently in the nest. Reluctantly he did just that and backed off slowly. The babies squeaked and here came the mother running. She grabbed one at a time in her mouth and carried them off safely to a new hiding place. Kelly said grinning, "Now aren't you glad you didn't hurt the babies? I knew their mother would be so happy to them." He was always kind and not a mean bone in his body. We never went mice hunting again.

While the boys played together sometimes I would go to their home and play with their sister. She was pretty and her Mother was always nice to me. We all walked to school together. Kelly always watched his sister and I cross the busy street safely every school day. Our new friend in the neighborhood was a real hero in my eyes.

One of the scariest times I remember was the day when we returned home from playing with the neighbor kids. Aunt Mary was standing in the yard looking very upset and nervous. She asked us if we had seen Francie anywhere. She then explained they were taking a nap together and when she woke up our sister was gone. She had looked every where inside and out but could not find her, and was frantic. We assured her not to worry we knew she didn't go out of the yard or at least not far from the house. Ronald said, "We will find her." We started looking by going next door. "Have you seen little Francie?" we asked Jennie. She answered, "She isn't very far away, look in the high grass and you will find her." We were sure she was right so we hurried to the high grass and caught a glance of a newspaper blowing above the grass and heard a child talking. I just knew finally we had found our sister. Pretending to be reading the paper did not surprise us as she was a great one to make believe. I asked her why she was out here all by herself. She explained the best she could that she wanted to read the paper and look at the pictures. A picture of a cute little dog encouraged her to ask if she could have a dog. I said, "Maybe you can have a kitten too. Now lets go back home to see Aunt Mary. She has been very upset looking for you." I took her little hand and let her into the house. Aunt Mary picked her up, hugged and kissed her like she had been gone for a year. She hugged and kissed Ronald and I also and told us we were really a good brother and sister to find Francie. To celebrate she asked my brother to bring a bottle of homemade root beer from the basement. We were still having a special party happy as we could be when Dad came home. After we told him what had happened he became very strict. He gave us orders not to dare go anywhere without asking him or Aunt Mary ever again.

Our Aunt reminded us so much of our mother, with her long red hair and loving ways. Ronald tried to please her, doing his chores without complaining and helping around the house. Being the oldest I'm sure he missed our Mom much more then I knew at the time.

It took a long time to truly realize Mother was not coming home so it was a blessing to have such a wonderful Aunt that loved us very much. What good memories I have of the time she spent with us. I have loved her all my life.

Dad began advertising for a housekeeper. Not many women wanted the responsibility of taking care of 3 children and doing house work. It was time for Dad to take a few days off his job to drive Aunt Mary back to West Virginia. She was getting a little homesick and we knew she could not stay forever. We had only a short time to visit before we had to start back. It took a while for Dad to choose the right person for our housekeeper before we left for West Virginia. Another hard time in my life would begin after returning home.

Soon after we were home, here came our first housekeeper. Mrs. Harris and her young son moved in with us. Well, needless to say as an only child he was very spoiled or that's how I remember him. All of our toys somehow became his. She always made us give into him.

Of course we didn't like that much, and she did not last long.

The next one was a young Seven Day Adventist, her name was Tibby. She was real good to us, and we started going to church with her. It was about a mile walk but we liked going so it was worth it. She didn't stay all night and that didn't work out too well. We liked her very much and thought she was too good to be true. I think from what I observed my Dad became too fond of her but she did not feel the same, so she gathered her belongings and started walking to her home. I think Dad had a little too much of his blackberry wine that night. We all jumped in the Model T and followed her down the street. Driving along beside her Dad begged her to not quit. He could not make her change her mind. We felt a great loss but off she went.

Spring time had arrived and so did Granny Smith the next challenge for us. She liked Dad's homemade blackberry wine. His stash was in the garage behind locked doors. Secretly Granny would give one of us a nickel to dig under the edge of the garage's dirt floor and get her a cup of his wine. Finally Dad began to wonder where his wine was going. One day he came home early from work and saw me crawling out from under the garage. At last he knew where his wine had gone. To complicate the situation, he found out from one of the neighbors that Granny was spreading the rumor that she was going to marry Dad. Another house keeper hit the road as we would say at the time. We were sorry about losing her because we liked her very much.

After a while Dad decided to drive to West Virginia to bring back another house keeper that was willing to try out the job. We finally reached Petroleum and started out the long ridge to the farm when all at once a tire went flat. After traveling most of the day we were so excited to be this close to our Grandma's. I thought to myself, why did this have to happen? Dad tried to get the tire off the rim but couldn't without the right tools. We kids were standing in the dusty dirt road when suddenly we heard a car coming. Dad looked up and said, "By golly I think that's your Uncle Guy, wonder why he's here?" I am sure his brother was as surprised as we were. He lived just next door to us in Akron and neither of the brother's knew about the others plans to drive home to their mother's farm that weekend. He put on his brakes and asked Dad what had happened and if he could help. Well, he went to his car and returned with a tool he had invented to pull a tire off the rim. Like a lot of men during that time you had to figure things out for yourself. There were few stores that sold tools but not a one out in the country. A flat tire did not slow us down much, thanks to good old Uncle Guy coming to our rescue. Grandmother was glad to see all of us arriving safe and sound. She was sure tickled to see her other son step through that kitchen door, she wasn't expecting him. It was a pleasant surprise for all of us. She had a warm supper ready for us. Those feather beds felt especially comfy that night.

We had just a few days to stay at Grandma Lewis' farm. She was the shepherd of her flock of sheep. There was always a lamb that was rejected by its mother needing extra care. My Aunt Belle would bring it to the house to bottle feed it in order for it to survive. We were outside in the front yard ready to leave when I spied Aunt Belle feeding a little lamb it's bottle. I ran over and begged to try and feed it. She finally gave in and warned, "Now hold onto the nipple real tightly as the lamb pulls hard on it." What do you know! When I started feeding him he sucked that nipple right off the bottle and it disappeared. He swallowed it! I was ready to cry when my aunt assured me that the lamb would be alright. It must not have been the first time that happened, I thought. We had such fun times watching our family milking cows, gathering eggs and feeding sheep as well as all the other farm animals. Watching Grandma ride side saddle on her beautiful horse and wondering how in the world she stayed on him. Good times had to end when we picked up our next housekeeper Aung Mag a distant relative. She was a bit older than the previous ladies. That might be one of the reasons why Ronald did not behave well and maybe I didn't either. One day we went over to a neighbor''s without permission. She sent for us but we didn't pay any attention and stayed for a long time. When we got home she was waiting for us. With a fly swatter she really laid in to both of us. I complained that it wasn't my fault but she said I should have come home without him. I knew she was right so I tried to obey her better and we didn't leave without asking for awhile. She did not stay too long. Dad decided things were not working out as well as expected, so back to West Virginia she went. It seemed to be the story of our lives; she left like all the rest.

During those few years living in Akron without my Mother and trying to endure the many changes in our life, I did survive. Many times I would think, if only Mom was here but my Dad tried his best and he was alone also. I have many memorable times and a lot of fun experiences I will share with you.

I remember one time feeling quite lonesome and missing my Mom a great deal. That is when I decided to visit Mother's good friend down the street. Since my brother didn't want to play with me that day I was really disappointed. The boys wanted to do things just boys did, and he wanted to play with his friends, not me. I asked the housekeeper if Francie and I could visit Mrs. Syphert. She asked me where she lived and I pointed down the street and she said for us not to stay too long. Mom's friend was so glad to see us and said she would like to talk to me. She said, "You know you are growing bigger and you should stop playing with boys so much. Little girls should stay inside and play together. You should be playing more with your little sister." I replied after thinking about what she had said, "I love her very much and I guess we could play house with our dolls, play store, or I could read story books to her. I'll ask Daddy to buy us some crayons and coloring books, which will be fun." She said, "I'm sure that is what your mother would like you two girls to do." I told her I really loved her and would do what she told me. My little sister loved playing house. We grew much closer during those times and we became the best of sisters forever after. Even though I liked playing inside I still could not resist playing most of my time with my ornery brother outside.

Easter time at Mrs. Syphert's was a delight. Her whole house was decorated beautiful. It reminded me of our house when Mother was still with us. A table full of little baskets full of jelly beans, chocolate eggs, little chocolate rabbits and fluffy yellow checks lying around. How excited I was, it all looked so delicious. I quickly reached out before thinking and put a jelly bean in my mouth. I immediately knew that it was wrong and almost cried. Mrs. Syphert came back in the room and handed me three bags of candy and said they were for Ronald, Francie and I. I wanted to tell her about eating one of the jelly beans without asking but I was too afraid and ashamed. I thanked her and left feeling very guilty that I had stolen something that wasn't mine. I cried about it and certainly regretted it but it was a lesson learned by a little girl early in life. I never took anything that didn't belong to me ever again.

I especially recall another time that summer when I was 7 years old. It was a dreary day and I was so lonesome thinking, why did my mommy have to leave us and go to Heaven? I decided that it might be a nice day to visit Mr. Syphert again. She had always been so good to us kids. Chester her son played with my brother but I did not have a girlfriend to play with. Only one thing made me hesitate and that was an old, ugly, white English bulldog that lived on that block. I looked down the street and couldn't see any sign of him. He must be inside I thought, so I'm safe. I walked fast and quietly and was almost past his house when he jumped off the porch and came running down the walk. Screaming at the top of my lungs, the lady of the house came up to the screen door and yelled, "He won't hurt ya!" Not believing a word she said, I put on more speed and ran onto Mrs. Syphert's porch, out of breath. "What is wrong child, was that gentle old bulldog trying to get you honey?" With a scared to death look on my face I said, "Well he is so ugly I can't help but run."" "OK honey, she said I will walk you around the block the other way when you're ready to go home." That night I dreamed of that old, ugly bulldog running after me over and over again. The next morning though I knew I would never have to go by his house ever again because I knew the back way around the block thanks to Mrs. Syphert.

One of the funniest things happened to my brother. Our father liked to hunt. One evening while he was out he found an owl's nest with a little white scared owl in it. He rescued it by bringing it and brought it home. When he showed it to us we were so excited to see an owl up close especially a cute little baby. Dad set some strict rules and said, "Now you three lads are not to go to the basement unless I go with you." He went downstairs and made a small cage out of chicken wire; put a lid on it but no lock. That was a big mistake! We obeyed for a day or two but the curiosity was too much for Ronald. We followed him down the steps into the dark, damp basement with its dirt floor. With a flashlight brother peered at the sleeping little owl, or so he thought. All of a sudden the baby owl fluttered and flew towards the light upstairs. We all screamed running up the stairs. That scared the owl even more. Flying around in the living room it was desperately trying to find a place to perch. Finally he settled down after perching on the edge of a framed picture. Ronald wasn't pleased so he punched at it with a broom. It promptly flew down and perched right on the top of Ronald's head. I never saw him so still. Now he was the one scared with his red hair standing straight up and tears running down his cheeks. Daddy, Daddy was all he could say but he would not be home for about an hour so he kept sobbing. Francis and I stayed real still not to disturb the owl. Imagine a kid with an owl perched on his head. It was pretty funny but not to dear brother. After about a hundred years, or so it seemed, we hear Dad coming on the porch. Francie and I rushed to tell him the bad news. Dad walked over slowly and took the owl by its feet and loosened the claws then took it back to its cage. Ronald sat down and quit crying ready for his punishment. Dad pointed his finger and said, "You see what trouble you get into when you do not listen to me?" We never saw the owl again, that night he took it outside and let it fly away. In just a few days

Ronald was again into mischief and I was right behind him.

One morning on our way to school a big ditch digger machine was hard at work making a lot of noise. The operator was cleaning the drain ditch on our street. My brother had to stop and watch of course, right in the middle of the street where the dirt was being dumped. The driver did not see him and kept dumping the dirt covering Ronald. He was covered to his knees and couldn't get out. I ran as fast as I could, throwing my hands up and jumping up and down at the driver. He didn't pay any attention for a while but finally stopped and asked what was wrong. I pointed to Ronald who by then was mostly covered up. He then saw his head sticking up and quickly got his shovel and dug him out of that dirt pile. While brushing him off he gave him a good hard talking to about what could have happened. Glover school was about ten blocks for us to walk. We stayed close to one another because it was a long way for me to walk but he never held my hand. We continued on to school that day but didn't tell anyone about the morning incident. If I had not been with my brother that day we might have never known what had happened to him. Although, we found out later the neighbor girl was watching from her upstairs bedroom window. On the way to school that day she sang Bye, Bye Blackbird a popular song of the day, but we didn't know at that time what she was trying to tell us. Ronald begged me not to tell Dad. I never did confess the many secrets we had, but maybe I should have.

Our Father would walk all three of us kids down the street to the Acme grocery store. They gave tickets each time you made a purchase that you could redeem for prizes. It took Dad a long time to get enough tickets to claim a little red wagon. It was a nice size, just right to haul our groceries home. One time when Dad was in a big hurry to go to Acme he left all of us at home. Of course we could not just sit around and wait for his return. On the next block men were building three story houses. One of the houses was close by and they had just finished the basement. Dad cautioned us before he left not to go near the construction. He might as well told us to go play there because we were too curious and couldn't resist the temptation. We waited until he was out of sight and away we went running as fast as we could because we knew we didn't have much time to explore. The men had quit working so no was around. There was a big board going down into that deep dark basement the one way in and the only way out. Ronald started down with me at his heels but we had to help our sister Francie with her short little legs. There was water and mud everywhere. We tromped around till we had our shoes and clothes really muddy. How were we going to explain this predicament? Ronald climbed up and looked around and saw Dad coming down the street pulling the red wagon full of groceries. He hollered at me and I came up but Francie couldn't make it alone. We started running for the house when I heard a woman scream, "Don't you two leave your little sister down there." We turned around and pulled Francie up the board and all three of us ran for our lives. Why were we so foolish to think Dad wouldn't know where we have been, we had evidence all over us. He looked at us and said, "You lads did the very worst thing I told you not to do, aren't you ever going to listen to me?" We knew we should have been good but we rarely were. I remember he made hamburgers for supper that night. I watched how he put bread crumbs, two eggs, salt, pepper, and chopped onions in a bowl then stirred in the hamburger. They sure tasted good. As usual, he gave us all a good bath and put us to bed.

My brother was always getting into trouble. Of course where he led I would follow. On this cold spring day he said we would ride down the big hill on E. Crosier St. as fast as the wind. Well off we went, him pulling our little red wagon and me walking as fast as I could beside him. Arriving at the top of the hill we saw men working on the street and big piles of sand on the sidewalk. They stopped and watched my brother get into the wagon and then I climbed quickly behind him. The wagon started to roll and picked up speed. Yes sir, we were going fast as the wind. It was really scary, but instead of going straight down the sidewalk he steered it into that sand pile. What a jolt! The wagon stopped instantly in the sand pile but I flew up over his head. I didn't remember anything for a short time. I guess everyone watching was afraid because I heard someone yell, "Is she dead?" Finally I staggered to my feet and picked up my hat. Then foolishly again I climbed in behind my brother and away we went. In the background we could hear the workmen laughing real loud. We made it to the bottom and flashed across the street and into our driveway. Good thing no cars were coming. I almost forgot Mom was gone for awhile, but then I remember wishing Mom could see us now! Maybe she did and somehow was watching over us that day. We felt mighty lucky that day and never told anyone about our day of adventure. If our Mother had been there she would never have allowed us to stray out of our own back yard.

We did not have a pet so all the kids in the neighborhood kind of adopted Trixie. She was our neighbor's dog that we loved and played with every day. She was a small, friendly, brown and white shepherd dog.

She always gave us a warning when the ice man was coming down our street. The ice wagon was pulled by a lovely mare that trotted down the street and always knew what houses to stop at. Trixie would bark giving us the signal to run out and meet the ice man. He would open the back doors of wagon then clamped a 25 pound of ice with a big hooked prong and throw the ice over his shoulder. He then delivered it straight to the customer's ice box. No such thing as refrigerators in our neighborhood. After he was paid he returned to the wagon and always chiseled off ice for all the kids and Trixie. What a treat on those hot summer days. When he left, his horse was running pretty fast and then we saw Trixie chasing the wagon. Somehow she got caught in the back wheel and was thrown out into the street and we just knew she was hurt really bad. When we reached her she couldn't get up, her hind leg was broken. Her owner picked her up and took her to her dog house. People took care of their own animals because back then because there were not many veterinarians. It took a long time for her to heal but we still loved her even with a limp. She never did chase after the ice wagon again.

It was a winter weekend and Dad was home so he made us stay inside. All of us were restless and were not very happy being cooped up. I had a secret and did not want to tell anyone. My little secret got so painful that Dad began to notice that I was crying off and on. Finally he asked me what I was crying about. Of course I didn't want to tell him, I knew he would give me a really bad scolding. By evening I was crying and just couldn't stop. He picked me up on his lap and said he wanted to know what was wrong. Well I told him there was something up my nose and it was hurting really bad. He turned me upside down and took the flash light and looked up my nose. There is something up there! Now you tell me what it is and how it got there. I hesitated but had to tell him that it was a shoe button and I had pushed it up my nose. Dad was very upset. I wondered how he would get a hold of it to pull it out. I explained it was a shoe button with the wire on it. "Well I'll get the button fastener and see if it can be pulled out," he said. He then turned me upside down again and told me I would have to hold real still. Brother Ronald held the flash light while Dad looked up my nose to see what he could do. It was so sore I almost cried but I wanted to get that button out of my nose. It was easy to pull out once Dad got it hooked. Oh boy, it sure did feel good when I saw it hanging on the end of that fastener. I had heard a saying, it's better out than in, and I have never forgotten that all my life. I rubbed my nose and gave Dad a kiss. Then I joyfully danced around the room. He told me, "Don't you ever put anything up your nose again,"" then looked at my brother and sister and said with a stern voice "that goes for you lads too." I have never forgotten his advice.

Doctors were few and far between but we had one of the best right at home. All three of us kids were pretty healthy youngsters most of the time. Whenever we were sick our Dad became the doctor on call. He had his own way of doctoring us. I can't remember ever going to a real doctor. If he would hear just a sniffle out of us he would get busy with one of his favorite cures, Vicks Vapor Rub. In our cold upstairs bedroom we would be ordered to strip down to our long underwear. Dad had a big flat bottle of Yeager's liniment. It was so strong when he pulled the cork we covered our faces with a towel. One at a time we would lay over his lap and he would rub us down with that stinky stuff. Quickly we would pull our underwear up and head down to the warm wood burning stove. Each of us would hold our feet up so Dad could rub them with Vicks. After our feet were well roasted we put on our socks and run as fast as we could up the steps to our beds.

One of the happiest days I can remember is when Dad spoke up an asked us if it was about time to make home made root beer. All three of us were yelling yes, yes because root beer was our favorite drink. We started to get our supplies ready. We needed a big five gallon crock jar, sugar, root beer extract, and three cakes of dry yeast. We hurried and carried our big crock out of the basement and gave it a good washing. We read his directions and Dad mixed the ingredients. About half the water was poured in the jar, then the sugar, stirring it real good. After that the root beer extract was poured in with the rest of the water. Last ingredient was three cakes of yeast. The jar was then covered with a plate and left to brew for about a week. Ronald kept a close eye on it daily to be sure it was brewing. We had to buy half pint bottles with caps that sealed. We had a bottle capper that pressed the cap onto the bottle top. It was a family tradition we really looked forward doing together. Then we put this special drink in the basement to age and cool so it would taste good. We would do anything to get a bottle of that special treat to enjoy. The only time we could have a bottle of that good old fashioned root beer is when Dad gave us permission and that was a very strict rule. Every time we went to West Virginia Dad took a generous supply to the family. Aunt Mary was always grateful because she especially loved our home made root beer that she had enjoyed when she had stayed with us in Akron.

When Dad was in a good mood, he was a lot of fun. He didn't have much of a social life working six days a week at Goodyear. This morning was a good Sunday for him. He decided to see if any of us three kids could dance. He got his harmonica out of his pocket and started playing, and then he started dancing the two-step. He sure was good at both of them. I went over to him and started tapping my feet. I could move only one foot at a time. Francie tried but it didn't work for her either. Ronald wouldn't try anything unless food was involved. I told Dad that I only two feet, one for dancing and one for church. He seemed to think that was real clever and a good answer. I don't think he realized that it took a lot of practice to learn to dance well. He and his brothers had had a lot of spare time in the evening growing up so they danced, while their sisters had school lessons or chores to do for their mother.

On another Sunday afternoon while riding in our Model T we had a comical happening. Although I'm sure the ladies involved didn't think it was funny. That day started with my brother, sister and I going to the United Brother Church. Our family used to attend together when Mother was still with us. We had to walk up the steepest hill in the neighborhood. Up Fifth Avenue hill we walked and down the other side to get to the church. Dad didn't go anymore for some reason but he wanted us kids to go. When we arrived home he always had a good dinner waiting. After my sister and I washed the dishes and cleaned everything up there wasn't much to do the rest of the day. After a short while Dad asked us if we wanted to go for a little ride. Of course we all agreed. As usual Dad had his glass of his homemade wine before we left. I hurried to the back seat with Ronald. Francie was so small she couldn't see anything unless she sat in the front. Everything went fine until a big fancy car stopped in front of ours. Dad said with a grin, ""I'm going to see how close I can get to that car without touching it!" He didn't look to steady to me but he drove real slow. All at once he bumped the car accidentally of course. I saw two women in the back seat through the cellophane window. When the car was hit they were lifted straight off their seat. Their beautiful big hats went flying off their heads and it looked so funny to me, but I didn't laugh even though I wanted to. The driver walked to the back of his car to observe the possible damage. Apparently there was no damage because he quickly drove away without saying a word. When Dad looked over our car low and behold the fenders were bent over the front wheels and we couldn't move. He looked desperate when he reached down and pulled on one of the fenders and it did not budge. He stood there for a short time trying to figure out what to do. Putting both legs on the tire he pulled the fender with all his might. It began to slowing straighten out and come free of the tire. After doing the same thing to the other side we drove quietly home. Later that evening he said that he was sure glad no one was hurt. He did drive a bit more careful after that but unpredictable things happen. I always wondered about those lovely ladies smashed hats and if they were ever able to wear them again.

Another little accident happened on another Sunday afternoon. We were driving down Arlington Street, just as a small church congregation was being dismissed. At that time, 1927 there were no traffic lights to give direction to traffic or pedestrians. Dad had slowed down but hadn't stopped. Suddenly a man came running across the street in front of my Dad's car. Of course he didn't have time to stop so we hit the man with a thump! I can remember the man flying straight up in the air and coming down with a thud in the middle of the street. Dad was really upset and rushed to help him stand up. When he stood up all his clothes fell off except his underwear. Dad asked him if he was hurt and he said no. He got him in the car before a crowd gathered. Dad asked him if he could take him to our place where they could talk things over. We all went quickly into the house where Dad again asked if he was hurt. The man again said no. "Well then I must find you some of my clothes to wear," our Father said. After he was properly dressed they started talking. The man said he would like to notify his wife but at that time we didn't have a phone. Dad said he would drive him home if this was agreeable to him. "What can I do to make it right with you? You know that you walked out in the street in front of my car and I had the right of way." He answered, "I know, I am sorry but that was my new suit and it was the first time I ever wore it." "I'm willing to buy you a new suit and give you $25.00 extra" Dad said. The man was thinking it over. ""Well, it wasn't your fault so I will take your offer," he replied. It was settled then and there. That's how things were settled between men back then, an agreement and a hand shake. Dad was smart and they both felt they had a fair agreement. After we took him to his home they planned the day that Dad would take him to buy the new suit he had promised him.

It was the fall of the year and a pretty nippy day. I was sitting on the back steps when Dad came out of the house. He told me he was going to pick apples for our winter supply. He asked me if I wanted to go with him, I said no I wanted to stay home. I thought why I should I go, as I continued to sit there. "We will have a good time picking apples!" he said with a twinkle in his eye. I will never understand why I didn't want to go. He asked me again and I said no. Well he got in the Model T and drove away. I wished he would have driven around the block, by that time I had changed my mind. I could have met him at the end of the driveway but he was gone. I cried and cried. He must have been gone at least two hours. When he drove up the drive he knew I had been crying. He told me I would have had a good time and I then realized what I had missed. I helped him carry all those beautiful golden delicious apples, my favorite, into the winter storage area in the cellar. The smell of those apples always brings back memories and regrets. Not going with Dad that day to pick apples is one of my greatest regrets of my childhood.

We all missed our Mother. I think Father's grief of losing his beloved wife Ella was much deeper then we could fathom at the time. He tried many times to hire someone to help him with the responsibility of taking care of us. After many disappointments he decided to try one more time. It was the fall of 1927. She was a young girl right out of high school and needed a job. It was mostly a baby sitting task because she didn't prepare our evening meal. She went home on the weekends and I was glad when Friday night came because it was the last night I had to sleep with her. I did not like sharing my bed. One of the neighbor men told my father that he had seen her at one of the public dances. He said she was wearing some right beautiful dresses. One of them had beads for decorations and was especially pretty. After that conversation Father became suspicious. He went upstairs and looked in the cedar trunk where Mother's clothes were stored. He discovered the most expensive dresses were missing and a few of her accessories. This made him very upset. The minute she arrived on Sunday evening he confronted her about stealing the clothes and asked her why would she do such a thing. She denied it until he told her someone had seen her at a dance wearing Mother's dresses. Looking ashamed, she admitted taking the clothes because she did not have anything pretty to wear and she wanted to look nice. He didn't give her any sympathy and told her he couldn't trust her and to bring back the clothes back right away. When she returned with my Mother's dresses he told her she could not work for us and to never again come back to our home. That is when I think my Dad decided to consider making other arrangements. There were other possibilities and maybe we would be better off and much happier. For about three stressful years trying to raise us with little help or success from multiple housekeepers he knew now he had to make a change in our lives.

Chapter Three
Living at Grandma Lewis' West Virginia Farm

OUR FATHER TALKED THINGS OVER WITH his mother about the problems he was having trying to work and raise us alone. After some thought she came up with an idea and Dad decided to consider her proposal. They made an agreement for our family to move back to West Virginia to her farm. We would leave Akron when school let out in June 1928. It was unfortunate that Dad had to give his notice to Goodyear Tire and Rubber Company after thirteen years of service, but things just hadn't worked out as well as he had hoped in Akron. He felt he had to do what was best for his family. No more housekeepers would be needed from here on out. It was a generous offer given to us by my Grandmother because it would mean four more family members living with her. Aunt Belle and her son Bob were already staying there since Grandpa had passed away two years earlier. It would take a lot more food to feed four more but thank God, that was one thing that was plentiful on the farm, vegetables, fruit, and meat. There was a great need for a good worker on the farm and Dad would fill those shoes. I understood she offered him a dollar a day for each day he worked for her. We could all stay in the big house until he had enough time to build us a small home close by on the farm. They agreed to talk things over again after the move. When the time came Grandmother came to Akron to help prepare and pack up all our belongings that we were going to take with us. She bought me a green silk dress, my sister a pretty blue one and brother some new clothes also. I guess she wanted us to look nice. Our Mother would have been pleased. Grandma went back home on the train so she could prepare for our arrival.

Right before we were ready to leave we crossed the street to say goodbye to our wonderful friends. Bert and Mabel Glaze had taken care of us when Dad was making arrangements for our Mom years ago. We thought we would never see them or their kids again but fate would work that out. Father's sister was married to Uncle Bernard and he had a big truck. Lucky for us he came to help take us all back to West Virginia. Ronald would ride with him and Francie and I rode with Dad. We forgot to take drinking water in our rush to get on the road. When my uncle got thirsty we stopped by a small creek and he took himself a big drink. Dad warned him not to and he would not let us kids drink from the creek even though all of us were very thirsty. Two days after we arrived, Uncle Bernard took typhoid fever and almost died. The priest came to give him last rites but Aunt Net would not let him come in the house, she chased him off and told him her husband was not going to die. It was a miracle he lived. His recovery took all summer but he was back driving his old truck in the fall. Moving from city streets to country roads was quite a change but I just knew it was the right decision.

That evening after a long trip following the loaded truck with everything we possessed in the world, we drove up the bumpy road. There it was Grandma's big beautiful farm house high on the top of the hill. We were all exhausted, and after eating our meal off to bed we went. All four of us had to sleep in one big bedroom. My brother and cousin Bob in one bed, and Francie and I shared another. Aunt Belle tucked us girls in first then the boys. She stayed with us until we fell asleep. That very first night I knew we were going to be happy about our move, there was only one thing missing; Mom. The next morning the rooster woke us up early with his cock-a-doodle-do. Our lifestyle was going to change starting this very first day at the farm. After breakfast we were anxious to wander around outside. I was looking through different eyes now. I was not just visiting for vacation; this was going to be my home. In a few days after unloading the truck and getting used to the new surroundings Grandma assigned our chores. Francie and I were to make all the beds and help inside the house. Another fun job for us was to feed the chickens and gather their eggs. Ronald and Bob were close to the same age so whatever chores Dad asked them to do they could work together. The day finally arrived when we got to meet our many cousins.

It wasn't long before we spied visitors coming up the winding hill to get acquainted with the new arrivals. What a wonderful surprise, it was Grandmother's sister and her five children! Clarence was sixteen, Carl fourteen, Dallas twelve, Sally eleven and Evelyn Doris eight. It was really exiting to have other girls living at the foot of our hill that we could play with. They became our very best friends. Their mother, Aunt Minnie was always really nice to us. Cousins bonded like brothers

71

and sisters because we spent so much time together back in those good old days. Farm country was a safe place to live. I never worried about running down the hill to play with my cousins. Everyone was trust worthy and watched out for one another. The month of June passed very quickly. Before I knew it July had started and the excitement began.

The farmers always looked forward to this special summer day, all work was forbidden. It was July 4th, 1928 in West Virginia a special historical event. There seemed to be contests among the men to create the most elaborate and exciting fireworks in the neighborhood. The men could only use their imagination to concoct fireworks from their farm supplies. Our father was a great cobbler and could always gather up most anything he needed for his clever mixture to produce fireworks.

All the grandchildren were not allowed to go near the barn where Dad worked on his project. I never knew what he used to make his fireworks it was his secret. Grandma's farm was on top of the highest hill and could be seen by all the neighbors. All would be watching her farm when the celebration started. On the afternoon there was so much excitement that the children had to be sent to the front yard and told not leave, Grandmother was afraid that they might get hurt. I think she was excited also, but tried not to show it.

About 7 o'clock the event started. We had plenty of apple cider that had been cooled in the cellar. Our two boys Ronald and Bob always had to go to extremes drinking the cider. Cousins Clarence, Carl and Dallas were visiting that day also. Aunt Belle was watching and knew what was happening so she removed the almost hard cider and replaced it with milk. The big boys didn't like the milk but all us little kids were in our glory. For extra flavoring sugar and cinnamon was mixed with the milk and it was delicious. Everyone liked it then, even the big boys.

It seemed to take a long time before dusk arrived. As a 10 year old girl I was getting anxious for the big fireworks to begin. I spied over the fence and saw my Dad coming from the barn with torches. These were rags tied on one end of long sticks, kind of like broom handles. The rags were soaked in oil and used to light the end of a metal pipe that the fireworks were supposed to be in. Well, Dad had everyone's attention when he stuffed his secret mixture into the end of the pipe. I can remember watching him run faster then ever before, away from the explosive pipe. The fire from the torch set the pipe on fire and with a loud bang the pipe jumped into the air and spurted fireworks way up into the sky spreading the colorful explosion all around. How beautiful the fireworks were but they were also dangerous. When that red hot pipe fell down from the sky it made a huge hole in the ground. All of us kids screamed bloody murder and even Grandma put her apron over her head. It was quite a sight!

Out of no where the phone started ringing. Grandma ran to the house to answer it, the neighbors in the valley below were calling. They said all them watched the pipe and fireworks blow high in the sky. Others called and said they saw the celebration display from a long ways off. We watched when their displays shot off but they didn't come close to my Dad's amazing fireworks. Dad asked Grandma if he could put off one more, and he again showed off another grand display. Grandma said, "Stop now, safety is the first rule." Everyone enjoyed the day even the people that lived far away from our farm. The 4th of July was over for this year but next year I was sure it would be bigger and better.

It wasn't all fun and good times at Grandmothers. Dad was hired to do the farm work and raise corn for the animal's winter food. He planted corn across the river on the other farm and he needed help to hoe the rows. The two boys Bob and Ronald were enlisted for that job. I was to ride the horse and steer him through the rows to keep Dad plowing straight, otherwise the horse would tromp on the corn. At the end of each row that big horse would step on at least three stocks of corn. No way was he a bit careful and I was blamed. How was I to keep him from doing that? Dad thought I could and of course it was always my fault when it happened. I was hot and sticky and getting a bad sun burn and I blew up at my Dad. I talked back to my Dad and said, "If you weren't so stingy trying to use every inch of ground you would have some room for the horse to turn around. You know that he is going to step on them sooner or later and it is not my fault." He just stood there and didn't say a word. It was miserably hot and we were all tired. Dad said, "Guess we better quit for the day and start for home." Both boys grabbed their hoes and started for the wagon. I had to get down off the horse and take off my overalls so I would look decent if we passed anyone on the way home. Girls weren't supposed to wear boys clothes, so I would have been embarrassed if anyone had seen be in those ugly overalls.

Grandmother was surprised to see us home early but didn't ask any questions. Francie was delighted, she had missed me as she was used to us always being together. She had to play by herself now but loved playing with the cats and hound dogs. Aunt Belle liked having her around for company. I thought my sister sure was lucky that she was too young to work in the cornfield.

The following week Grandma asked me if I wanted to go berry picking with her and Aunt Belle. Well I thought I should give it a try since it might me fun. Blackberries were Grandma's favorite even though they grew in hard places to get to. We covered ourselves with long sleeve shirts, coveralls and heavy shoes. We were protecting ourselves from the thorns on the plants and especially from chiggers which was its own challenge. The thorns would cut into your skin and the tiny insect would crawl under your clothes getting under your skin itching you to death. Each of us had a small bucket attached to our belt with a rope. When you found a good patch you kept it to yourself so you could fill your bucket before anyone else. When filled I dumped the delicious berries into a large tin tub that was then carried to the wagon. At the end of the day when all the tubs were full we climbed up in the wagon and the horses pulled us home loaded with our treasure. Dad helped unload the tubs, and that was just the beginning of the hard work ahead of us. Early the next morning we carried water into the kitchen from the wishing well beside the house. I helped wash all the berries preparing them to be cooked. On top of the cook stove big kettles were filled with berries. Sugar was added then the batch cooked for a short time. All the canning jars were washed and ready to be filled with those purple delights. Filling and sealing at least one hundred jars for our winter supply would be worth all this effort. Canning was a necessity in the country. While we were working that day Grandma reminisced about the good old days when she took my Dad picking with her years ago. I really enjoyed her telling about his childhood when he was a boy. I never became tired of listening and enjoying hearing her stores. Grandma was part Indian and indeed knew a lot about the use of herbs and fruit for medicinal purposes. Berry juice was one of her best medicines for winter ailments. Sometimes I pretended to be a little sick just to get a drink of that sweet juice. Surprisingly I seemed to get better the very next day. Cherries were another fruit that was plentiful. There was a big tree in the back year close to the house. We had to keep a close eye on them when the cherries stared to ripen. Just as they started to turn red the robins would spot them. Birds would come in droves and devour all the cherries if we did not watch real close. Many times a day Grandmother would go out and shoot her twenty-two pistol into the air to scare them off. To no avail nothing we did saved most of the fruit. Those robbing birds were alert and had a feast. There were a few left for canning and a few cherry pies were baked from the left over''s.

In a few days Aunt Net visited. That was a common thing to happen, family members were always welcome. She brought her young son Alvin with her. The next morning Francie and I were strolling around the barnyard looking for something interesting to do. There was our little red wagon we had pulled our cousin in the day before to keep him from crying. We were all by ourselves and could choose to do whatever we wanted to get into that day. I asked her if she thought we could go for a ride around the hillside. She really thought it was way to steep and wouldn't be able to stop the wagon. I declared we could handle it and I would be careful. It was settled, being the oldest I climbed in the front and sis behind me. Away we went, slowly at first then the wagon picked up speed. Faster and faster we went. No way could I control red lightening now! I yelled for Francie to hold on tight because we were going to hit the rail fence. We crashed with a bang! We flew out and our red wagon was broken in three or four pieces never to be repaired. My knee was bleeding but my sister didn't have a scratch on her. She helped me up and we started up the hill. Grandma would have to know now as my knee needed bandaged. Just as we reached the barnyard there was Aunt Net standing there with Alvin in her arms. She asked us to please take him for a ride in our little red wagon again. We pleaded and told her we could not do that right now. Of course she wanted to know why. I told her to look down over the hill and she would know why not. She gasped, ""Oh my goodness what will you daddy say?"

We were thinking exactly the same thing. Grandma was not too surprised about the wrecked wagon and said that would be one less thing she had to worry about. Maybe she had expected a problem with a wagon and all those hills and children a little too adventuresome. I wasn't always the most obedient child in the family and certainly not perfect as I'm sure you've noticed! My Dad thought I was because good old Grandma didn't tell everything that happened when he was away. I was sure lucky that day!

That same month Dad was giving the house a new coat of white paint. All of us kids were standing under the ladder watching every stroke he made with his brush. He told us we were in his way and to go play somewhere else. He said it was dangerous with him on such a high ladder and he sure didn't need our help and for us to get lost. Boredom I guess is why we wandered down to the barn. The buck sheep was fenced in so he couldn't get out. Well that's what we thought. He was real mean to everyone but Grandma. She hand fed him grain and he ate it like candy. He was curious and watched every move we made. Trying to find a way out and get free was really what he was doing, trotting back and forth. With a stick we took turns punching at him and making him madder with each punch. Behind the barn we had found a half bottle of some kind of whiskey. One of the men must have forgotten about leaving it there. Someone came up with the idea to feed it to the ornery buck sheep. He drank it like a trooper then he really became lively. Ronald called the dog down to play with the buck. What a mistake! When the dog jumped in the pen they went round and round. The big buck sheep started running and flew up over the fence like it wasn't even there. We started screaming, and not knowing what had happened Father was off the ladder in a flash. He ran towards the barn and said he knew we had been teasing the buck sheep. He was upset with us because he had to stop painting and go after the buck sheep. He said it would be a hard task to catch him let alone drag him back to the pen. He ran across the back field and grabbed him by the collar and tried to make him walk back quietly but that didn't work. Dad picked up a stick and tried to coax him but that didn't work either. There were both pretty stubborn so Dad picked the buck up and threw him over the fence once there were close enough. The reason I can remember this exciting experience so well is that we were right behind Dad following his every step. I never wanted to miss anything. Grandma was watching and told Dad she was glad the old buck sheep wasn't hurt because he was the only one for miles around.

One of the most vivid things that stuck in my mind as a child was the first time I saw a corpse. During the summer one time Grandma's phone rang, and the message from the neighbor was not good news. The owner of our neighborhood store had passed away. The news spread like wild fire. I really felt I wanted to see Mr. Heck for the last time. He was always at the country store every time I was lucky enough for Grandma to take me with her. Everyone bought their groceries there and knew each other. He was the largest man in the neighborhood and one of the most popular politicians in the area. When our family and I entered his home I remember he was laid out on a large slab in the hallway. Because he was so large, a casket had to be built to bury him. The men were busy finding a crew to dig his grave at the Heck Cemetery. Most every family had their own private cemetery. There were different churches in the community and they all worked together when it came to chores like this one. All the neighbors attended the funeral including me.

I thought about him later and remembered when any children had came into his store he gave them each a stick of candy. He loved children. If any one could not pay for their groceries, he would give them credit with lots of time to pay their bill. He was certainly missed in the community for a long time. I never forgot him; he was one of the good guys. His wife kept the store going for a long time and then another family took it over. It was never the same going to the store after Mr. Heck was not there to wait on us. He was a nice man and knew to make you think you were a special person. It made him happy to make others happy. Everyone loved him and wasn't afraid to tell him so. He's a lesson for all of us on how we should treat those we love right here in our own families.

Occasionally our Grandmother on my Mother's side would call and want us to visit so Dad would drive us over the dusty roads to the Null's. It wasn't too far by car but way too far to walk. Our two double cousins lived with Grandma Null. Their names were Rhoda and Monelle, and they were about the ages of my sister and I. Our Father's each married sister's giving us the same set of grandparents and that's where "double" cousins came from. We were so close we really felt like four sisters. All of us loved each other very much. We played a lot of make believe games. That particular day we decided to ask Grandma if we could play in the small house where the hired hands lived. She knew the four of us were extremely nosey, but the nodded as if to say it would be OK. She then ordered us not to touch a thing. Not one thing of the men's belongings do you dare touch she repeated. The first thing that caught our eye was a lovely guitar. The temptation was too much. "Who will be the first one to try and play it", I asked? Neither one of our cousins was musical nor did Francie want to get into trouble. So I started stroking the guitar. It has a nice sound I thought. Rhoda suggested we play church. We all broke out singing the song, "Never Grow Old" in harmony. I seemed to be in charge so I asked, "Who wants to give a testimony?" Rhoda and Monelle did a good job trying to say things we had heard in church. It sounded nice to us, and I dismissed us in prayer. I put the guitar carefully back where we found it and slammed the door behind us. We were on a mission now to do the work of the Lord. On our way back to the house there was a dead toad on the path. Of course we had to have a funeral. The ground was so hard we couldn't dig a proper hole for its grave. Rhoda ran to the house and brought back a large spoon, and that worked just fine. We placed the toad on a bed of grass we gathered then covered him gently with dirt. We softly sang a hymn, and then burst out with "Onward Christian Soldiers" as we marched off towards more mischief. We always seemed to get in some kind of trouble when all four of us were together.

In the next week or two we came to Grandma Null's little house often. It was small and only had one floor. She had mirrors placed where she could see from one room to another. You could not have any secrets in her house because she saw everything. I didn't catch on to that for a long time. I always wondered how she knew everything I did.

We were all relaxing in the living room on this hot summer day. The women were all wearing dresses and just underwear to keep cool. Gazing out the front window I saw company coming down the drive. They were all dressed up in fine clothes. All the women but Grandma ran for the back bedroom to put their corsets on. They would not be caught dead without looking their finest. They all slipped on their corset and this under garment made them look much thinner! Not a young lady would go out in public without a corset on and always wore one when they had company. They were hot but it gave them a better shape so I guess they thought it was worth the discomfort. The visitors arrived and Grandma greeted them. She told them the rest of the family would be right in to visit. Aunt Mary wanted me to keep quiet and not tell about what they had rushed to do before the company reached the front porch. She told me to not tell everything I knew like I had done in the past. To keep me quiet she put a big corset on me and had me sit on the couch with just my head peeping out. I complained and told her to take it off of me. She did and told me to skedaddle and go outside and play with the company. I heard one of the ladies comment that I was an unusual child. No one in our family replied. The visitors stayed quite a long time and I thought they were planning on staying for supper. That would not be uncommon but they were not very well known by Grandma. Screaming was suddenly heard from outside. Their youngest boy had fell off the boardwalk and slipped into the creek below. He was not hurt but he was covered head to toe in mud. After all that excitement they decided to leave. That little accident saved Grandma from cooking a big meal. I was always blamed for causing that little incident but only admitted to bumping him accidentally of course. Grandma gave a sigh of relief when they drove out of the drive and said, "Thank God for little accidents even if they were intentional."

That evening Grandma Null asked me to dance for her before I went home. I was real excited she had asked me instead of one of the other kids that were there. I was hoping deep down that it was because I was her favorite. I tried to do my best, dancing with a flutter using my hands and feet moving together. Turning round and round and I then graciously bowed to her. She was very pleased clapping her hands and told me it was a lovely dance. I was a hit with the family! About that time Uncle Tome came in the room and asked me to dance for him. I reluctantly did my dance again. Grandma thanked me and told me I had danced the best for her. I replied, "That's because I love you the best!" When Dad picked my sister and I up to go back home I couldn't wait to tell him about my first dance.

Another afternoon at Grandma Null's farm when Uncle Tom came home from working in the oil fields he noticed his four nieces were up to no good. He was married to my Mother"s younger sister Grace and he was quite the tease. He watched us for a while running the chickens and trying to catch one with no success. "I"ll tell you how to catch a chicken and it's not by running after it. You have to throw salt on its tail," he instructed us. Gosh, we didn't know that, I thought! We squired off to the store house. Each of us filled a small bucket half full of salt. We started aiming for the chicken's tails but not one of them stopped after we hit our target. Uncle Tom was bent over hysterically laughing. We stopped and looked at him and instantly knew he had fooled us again. We were glad Grandpa didn't see us return to the store house and empty our buckets. We would have been in real trouble and maybe Uncle Tom too. Within seconds we were on to another project as if nothing had happened. We decided to make a playhouse out of an old empty corn crib. With an old broom we swept it clean as could be. Meanwhile our uncle was spying on us again. Empty boxes were our make believe chairs. Flowers were the next thing it needed. We picked wild flowers and put them in canning jars. It started to look pretty good to us. Just as we were getting settled along came someone pushing through the cracks with a big stick. They were trying their best to tear up our play house! All four of us started to scream at the top of our lungs. Aunt Grace saw what and who the problem was. She yelled out the back door and said, "Tom let those girls alone and get in here where you belong!" He grinned at his beautiful redheaded wife as he waved goodbye to us. Our uncle was very mischievous. He always teased us to cause a little excitement in our lives. We fell for his tricks every time because he was quite a charmer. Despite all his teasing, he was undoubtedly my favorite uncle.

After many visits to the Null family home I was finally back at Grandma Lewis's. Her magnificent four bedroom home on that high hill was my home now. I had become used to living in the country. I never did quit missing my Mother even though the family all treated me with loving kindness. Early one morning after breakfast I was skipping around the house counting cracks in the sidewalk. All at once I stopped and sniffed something familiar. The sweet smell of an apple pie baking filled the air. I knew Grandma was baking apple pies and I would get a piece soon. My mouth watered as I entered the kitchen screen door. Last week she was canning pickles. The aroma of spices and vinegar had tickled my nose. I had had the urge to eat a whole jar of pickles but I didn't. This week the chore of canning beans was at the top of the list. I heard the snap, snap, snap as Grandma was preparing the green beans for canning. I watched for a while but was anxious to snap a few beans myself. Finally I asked her if I could help but she told me it was a special job and I should go and play while she did the work. I agreed and made up a song as I strolled around the house. Snap, snap, snap jump the crack I sang. Blackie the big dog came running around the corner with his nose to the ground. He bumped into me and knocked me down and I scraped my knee on the cement. I screamed for Grandma telling her I was hurt and to come quick. Aunt Belle told me she jumped up and dumped the beans from her apron into the basket and came running to my rescue. She said to me, ""My child, are you hurt? Let me pick you up and take you inside. You know I"m part nurse too. I had nine children to take care of a long time ago. They were always getting hurt." I asked her if I was too big to cry and she confirmed ten year old girls are allowed to cry. She put some clover suave on my knee and wrapped it with a clean strip of white cloth. She fastened the bandage together with two of the safety pins from the string of pins she had fastened to her apron. She put me in a chair close by her and asked me if I felt better. It sure felt good watching her go back to stringing and snapping the green

84

beans. Hearing the sound of string, string, snap, snap, I begged her to let me help. She agreed mostly out of feeling sorry for me I'm sure. With a grin Grandma said she thought four hands were better than two so she would string and I could snap. Now we were partners. What a team I thought. We put them into a basket for Aunt Belle to get ready to wash for canning. Blackie crept over slowly and watched every move we made. He moved his head from side to side as we worked. I asked Grandma if she thought Blackie knew I was doing a good job. She said with a smile on her face that he was a mighty smart dog so I bet he thinks you're the best bean snapper he ever saw. Then I looked at Blackie and told him if it hadn't been for him I wouldn't have become the best bean snapper in West Virginia as I patted him on the head.

The canning was mostly done and my knee was healed before Aunt Ellen come to visit. She was the youngest of Dads sisters and favored by the family. Her son Charles was named after her father Charles Lewis. He was just as cute as a button. A chubby little guy and he loved everybody. I had the pleasure of playing and watching over him. He liked to run so I held his hand while we ran as fast as he could go around the house. I turned and looked behind us a saw a big snake crawling right where we had run. I started screaming snake, snake! Dad and my aunt were in the back yard visiting, and they came in a hurry. The snake was trying to crawl under the house for safety but couldn't find an opening. Dad rushed to the shed and brought back a hoe. He struck the snake but it didn't die until he cut its head off. He threw it over the fence and told us if there is one snake there is always the mate somewhere close. That was quite a scare because it was a copperhead snake and they are poisonous. That was the first time we had seen a copperhead on the farm and we never seen another one. Thank goodness the only snakes we saw after that were black snakes in the barn. They were never disturbed because their specialty was the mice in the barn that was eating our grain.

Aunt Belle sure was happy when her sister was there because that meant that someone could help her with the important chore of milking the cows. As they walked to the barn I trotted behind along with our four cats. The cats would line up beside each cow and wait for my aunts to squirt milk at them. One at a time they would open their mouths wide to drink their breakfast. Each evening the same thing would happen then they would sleep in the hay at night. It would take about an hour twice a day to milk four cows by hand. I tried to milk and only could get a cup of milk so that finished my milking career. We were sad to see Aunt Ellen and cousin Charles leave but our busy farm life continued.

Summer was ending, and for me it was a long anxious two or three weeks waiting for this day to arrive. It was time for our annual unusual visitors to come again. I would listen every day for them to come up our hill. "Here they come, here come the Gypsies," I excitedly yelled at Grandma. Our farm house was isolated from the main road but they never failed to find us each year. All week long Grandmother had been hearing from the neighbors that the Gypsies were camped a few miles down the road. I climbed up on the gate and stretched as tall as I could to get the first glimpse as the came around the curve in our road. Hearing the grinding and crunching of their iron rimmed buggy wheels started my heart beating wildly. Grandmother's favorite expression was "give them a good supply of food and be generous then they will not visit you during the night." I didn't know what that meant at the time. That is why she bagged up lots of potatoes, apples and other non-perishable produce for their expected visit. I was going to see for the first time real Gypsies with my own eyes. Swaying from one foot to the other watching big eyed and breathless I saw a skinny old horse slowly laboring up the hill pulling his heavy load. Every bone was showing and his hip bones looked as though they would come through his skin at any time. At last the horse stopped. Out of the large covered wagon one of the most beautiful girl I had ever seen jumped down. She had jet black hair, dark eyes and pearly white teeth. With a pleasant smile she helped the older lady step down from their carriage. They wore long black skirts that swished as they flounced through the gate. Their earrings dangled, bracelets tingled and on their hands were their many sparkling shiny rings. The older woman reached down and patted me on the head and told me I a beautiful one with my golden red hair. She said, "May you live in good health." I felt very blessed. Just then our watch dogs came around the house barking furiously. Grandmother came out of the house quickly and called the dogs. They obeyed her and quit barking immediately. My Grandma had cautioned me to watch our quests every move and I intended to do just that. There were all kinds of stories and rumors about food, chickens, piglets, and even horses missing after they left an area. Of course more details were added each time a story was repeated. Grandma greeted the older lady and said, "It is nice to se you again, Lyube. I hope you are in good health. Who is this lovely girl you have with you today?"" The old Gypsy looked pleased that her name had been remembered. She then presented her grand-daughter as Princes Ruba. I was introduced as Marjerie Texas as I curtsied. A nod of her head was my only recognition. Grandma asked them if they would sit and have a cup of tea. They looked at each other with surprise but accepted the invitation. They followed us into the parlor then Grandmother left us to prepare the tea and cookies. Ruba asked me if I liked visiting and I told her I was not visiting, I lived here and I took care of my Grandma. Out of the corner of my eye I noticed a quick movement from the older lady, I saw the little golden vase that was on the coffee table had disappeared. I wondered what I should do now. I made up my mind right away and said politely, "Excuse me, that golden vase belongs to my Grandma and it was given to her by my dear Grandpa and it is very special." I marched over to her with authority as I was talking. She stared at me with surprise and shame then took the vase out of the big pocket of her skirt. Immediately she polished it with her hankie and said, "Now it is bright and shiny for your Grandma." I was holding the vase when Grandma appeared with refreshments. I told her I was showing our guest her beautiful vase as I placed it back on the coffee table. The Gypsies were served with pomp and royalty. After tea they said they would have to be on their way. After loading their wagon with lots of baskets of fine produce Lyuba said, "Bless you and may no evil befall you or yours." I never saw Lyuba or Princess Ruba again and I never told Grandma about her precious vase. It was my secret.

I became bored again after the Gypsies left the area. Not too much was happening that excited me, life went on. Francie and I played most of the time outside together. We were out in the front yard when we saw our dog Spot carrying something in his mouth. I called to him, "Here Spot, come here you big old doggie." Our big collie dog came slowly and dropped s small furry bundle at my feet. Francie yelled, ""Gee whizz it's a baby rabbit and it is still alive. Lets take him in the house and take care of it." Grandma warmed milk then dipped her finger in it. Then she gently rubbed his mouth open. The wee baby liked it and wanted more milk. We didn't know where to keep him. A shoe box would make a nice nest we thought. Francie said she would get some grass to put in it for a bed, and Grandmother agreed. Next morning when we were washing breakfast dishes when Grandma came rushing in. She was out of breath and said for us to come quickly, our little rabbit was loose outside. Dropping everything we rushed out the kitchen screen door. Out in the meadow was Benji. My sister adored animals and always gave them a name. Well there he was nibbling on the sweet grass. I tip toed towards him slow and easy. Sister came through the gate and stood real still. He stopped eating and threw back his long ears then continued eating away. Benji looked at us then hopped a short distance. I eased closer; he flipped his ears and hopped a little further. I decided I would have to run him down to be able to catch him. That little rabbit zigged and zagged forward then backwards quick as a flash. I couldn't keep up with him. What a race! He hopped towards Francie, she waved her dish towel and back he hopped towards me. It was now or never. With one last burst of speed I leapt for Benji. Oh no, I could not get up, something was wrong! My sister reached for the baby rabbit. My black satin bloomers elastic had broken when I fell. I pulled them up but thought a safety pin would sure come in handy! As we went inside we all three were laughing and smiling, very pleased to have caught Benji. Francie carried the tired baby back to his shoe box bed. When she laid him down she shouted, "Grandma come look!" All curled up in the corner was our Benji but who was this other cute bundle we had caught? Grandma looked in the box and started to laugh. We all laughed and laughed. We decided they might be brothers, well just maybe!. Then Grandmother hugged us both and exclaimed, "I doubt if any other little girls could run down and catch a wild baby rabbit!" She told us we would have to turn them loose real soon. The next day we fed them while Grandma tied up Spot. She said it would be safe now to turn them free again in the meadow. We knew she was right. It was hard to do, but we did the right thing even though it was sad just the same. When we set them free they hunkered down in the grass, twitched their noses then stood on their hind legs looking around. It was if they were trying to decide what direction to run. They were zig-zagging back and forth then disappeared out of sight. I looked at Francie and saw big tears streaming down her face. I asked her not to cry. We could watch them play in the meadow every day. I told her that baby rabbits didn't want to be shut up in a box and neither would we. They will be happy with their family again. With a lump in my throat I explained all of this the best I could to my little sister.

Summer was slowly coming to an end. School would be starting soon. I sat by myself thinking about what a happy time I had during the last few months living in West Virginia. Moving from a small house in town in Akron, Ohio to a big country farm house seemed so long ago. I thought I was so lucky to live in a beautiful nine room house. The first floor had a kitchen, dining room, sitting room, bedroom and a parlor. I thought about Grandma with her parlor key, safe in her apron pocket and not allowing anyone to go in unless she invited them. The second floor had four bedrooms. One bedroom was always ready for the company we had during most of the summer. The large walk out porch on the second floor was a great place to see for miles. On the first floor porch was where we all rested in the evenings after a hard days work. I always looked forward to listening to my Dad tell about all the things he had accomplished each day. Grandpa Lewis had really planned a wonderful house when he built it for his family many years ago I thought. I wished my Mom was here, but she wasn't. I knew the summer months had went very fast and September would be here before I could blink an eye.

Chapter Four
Going From a City to Country School

SEPTEMBER ARRIVED AND IT WAS ALMOST time for school to start. I was anxious to see the inside of the small school my sister, brother and I would attend for the first time. We had walked by it many times in the summer but had no idea what the inside was like. The windows were too high to peek in so we were excited to see inside. A one room school house just could not compare with the nice brick school we had attended in Akron. It was modern with inside plumbing and lots of kids came for miles around. This building that looked like our country church was wood and not very big. How could it possibly compete when you had to go outside to two little buildings behind the school they called their bathrooms. One marked girls and the other one marked boys. The land was purchased by my Great Grandfather Dotson in nineteen hundred to build the first school house in the settlement named Rusk. My Father, his brothers and sisters all went to this school so I thought I should at least give it my best try. All the neighborhood children would start the same time as we would, first grade to eighth grade all in one room. It just couldn't possibly work, or that"s what I thought. How could one teacher teach all these classes? Well I guessed I would find out soon enough. What a surprise the little school turned out to be. Outside was a well with a hand pump where we would get our drinking water and clean up after recess.

It only had one front door to enter and exit. No electricity, no gas, just a big pot bellied stove for heat. As I entered I saw a cloak room with a small window and hooks on the walls for each child to hang their coats. On the floor there was a space to place goulashes in a line. By one window there was a large crock jar with a spigot, the drinking water for the day was stored in it. Beside it was a tin cup with a few dents in it that all the kids drank out of with no fear of passing germs. Desks were in two rows on each side of the room. In the middle was the large coal stove. The teacher's desk was at the head of the room with a long bench in front of it. Later I found out it was the recitation bench. Each grade of students had to sit up front together and answer the teacher's questions. Behind that desk were black boards with erasers and chalk on the rounded ledge. A large world globe was hanging up high in one corner. It was on a long chain with a pulley so the globe could be pulled down to eye level when needed. There was a library of about twenty five or thirty books in a cabinet with glass doors. We all found our seats according to our grade. I was in the fifth grade, Francie started in the third and Ronald in the seventh. Before school started my cousin Sarah tried to talk me into starting in the sixth grade with her. I refused; I knew I could not pass the test because I did not know fractions. I would have been so embarrassed because I had never failed a test.

Only twenty five students were our complete student body. Many of them were relatives making it much easier to make friends quickly. Walking up the rocky road to Grandma's house late that afternoon I had mixed emotions. The drastic change I had experienced the first day at the country school was different, but I thought I was going to like it. My eight year old sister was holding onto my hand tightly as we climbed the hill. She mentioned how she had really liked her first day at school and was eager to go again tomorrow. The next day we learned about the teacher's rules. Mr. Moore had been in the army so he was strict but also very kind. His son came to school with him but he never showed any favoritism. The first rule was no chewing gum, and then there was no fighting inside or on school grounds. Only the teacher could raise the windows and put the sticks under them to hold them up allowing cool air to come in when it was to warm. Another important rule was no one but my cousin could put coal in the stove. He was the janitor and old enough to be responsible for this job. I had always thought the most important rule was no cheating! I knew I would never cheat but I wasn't sure about the other students. We always had to hold our hand up to get permission to speak or make a trip outside to the outhouse.

We all had to salute the American flag and repeat the Pledge of Allegiance each morning. We would all recite the twenty third Psalms and say the Lord's Prayer together. Every one of us knew if we disobeyed our teacher we would be in deep trouble when we got home. Our parents respected Mr. Moore and backed him up on all his rules. If you misbehaved at school, you were also punished at home and that was my Father's rule. Recess was from ten thirty to eleven o'clock each day. We were supposed to use the outhouse during this time but most of us didn't. Playing tag, drop the hankie and blind mans bluff was much more important to us. Baseball was one of the favorite games but we did not have enough time for a full game, so it would be continued till the next day.

Occasionally in the evening there would be planned events such as debates, cake walks and community meetings. My brother had a reputation as one of the tough boys, Right after school started he acquired the nickname of "Fats". He was a big boy for his age, and Ronald was always in some kind of trouble. One day at recess I saw Harry, the biggest bully beating my brother on the ground. My temper went into high gear, and I jumped on Harries back beating him and scratching his face. He told all the kids he had been attacked by a tiger. From then on my nickname was "tiger"; I was somewhat a tom boy. At home I had to take up for my sister and I, Ronald would tease and pick on us when Dad wasn't around. I let him know we would not put up with his teasing, but I also knew if anyone else had picked on us he would have fought them like a wildcat. That's what brothers are supposed to do!

Within a few weeks we had the habit of walking to and from school together with our cousins. School let out about four o'clock and we all started walking towards home. Evelyn ran ahead of us and was in the middle of the road. Harry Shook, the oil driller was driving his model T Ford toward her. He couldn't stop when she ran out in the road suddenly, and his car hit her, knocked her down and ran over her. We were all screaming, and thinking she must be dead! There she was standing behind the car laughing. His old car came to a quick stop, and he jumped out shaking like a leaf. When he finally saw her standing there he asked her if she was hurt. She was so scared and had thought she was on the wrong side of the road, but she was ok. All the kids gathered around by then, he told her he would drive her home to explain to her father what had happened. We all pointed down the road to her house. Her father my Uncle Lemon was sitting on the swing on his front porch when we arrived. All the kids that could fit in the car including myself rode with Evelyn. Her father said there was no reason to take her to a doctor. He did not act one bit excited. Mr. Shook said it was an accident and to keep in touch if any complications set in. Of course nosey me could not wait to get home to tell Grandma before anyone else. The very next day guess who was driving slowly up the road and stopped? Mr. Shook got out and asked for the little girl he hit the day before. Evelyn came forward then and he handed her a large bag of stick candy. He said she could share it if she would like to. Boy was she instantly popular. We each choose a stick of our favorite flavor and thanked her for sharing. As we licked our sticks of candy I told her we were all glad she had not been hurt and that the accident had turned out to be a happy accident.

School days went past fast and weekends were filled with family time and going to church. I was learning all the necessary subjects. Reading, writing, arithmetic, geography, history and spelling was taught to every grade just at different levels. The teacher made a contest out of spelling, the subject I loved best. Once a week we had a spelling bee. Mr. Moore picked out a captain for each of the two teams. I was picked for the first team as captain, and my brother was picked for the second team. We were both good spellers. Our cousin Bob seemed to always be picked last, he was poor at spelling. All the kids were real excited trying to figure out who would win. If you could not or misspelled a word you had to sit down. The team with the most students standing won the game. It was a lot of fun and educational at the same time.

When the leaves on the beautiful trees started to turn color we knew fall was on the way. It would be a change to walk to school on those chilly days all bundled up with coats and boots. The school was real cold when we entered one fall morning. There was no sunshine coming through the windows so that made the building much colder than usual. Carl the janitor in charge of the coal stove was already there. He was trying but couldn't get the fire started. He was just about to give up when he remembered an old can of crude oil that was in the storage room. I never knew what got into him but he threw that oil on the hot coals, what a mistake that was! The big stove started to dance and shake wildly. The ten foot stove pipe came loose and bounced down on the floor just missing all us kids. The teacher was frantic, black soot covered the floor and most of our faces. What a sight! Flames shot out of the stove pipe. If the fire had blown out of the stove we would have been in real danger. Finally, the coal stove and the stove pipe started to cool down. Now what was the teacher to do? He was responsible for our safety. Mr. Moore began to collect his thoughts. I'm sure he wondered if he should have led us out of the building immediately out of danger. It had happened too fast and it was over now and thank God no one was injured which was the most important thing to him and me too. He asked Carl what possessed him to throw the oil on the coals. He replied with a lump in his throat, "All the kids were real cold and fire just wouldn't catch. I didn't think there were still hot coals in the stove." I felt very sorry for my cousin because I knew he didn't mean to cause such a disaster. The teacher still thought Carl should be punished by cleaning up the mess he created. Mr. Moore said he needed warm water, wash clothes and towels. Carl quickly volunteered to go the short distance to his house and bring back our needs. He scurried out the door and returned in just a few minutes.

The older girls washed the faces of the little kids, it didn't help much. We were told to go back home for the day, everyone but Carl. He stayed and worked hard scrubbing the floor and everything else that was covered with soot. Our parents were so thankful that no one was hurt. A few of them came to the school and helped Carl while others brought extra cleaning supplies. What a job that must have been. The next day was Saturday, and the neighborhood men offered to help put the stove pipe back in place. Monday the school house was nice and warm, filled with all of us kids there bright and early with clean shining faces. The school house tragedy was over but not forgotten. Days were getting colder and colder so recess activity as about over till spring. We had to look forward to the events that were held at school in the evenings. Cake walks were especially fun and all the women would bake a cake to bring. The money earned was donated for our school fund. Everyone would choose a partner and walk in a circle around the room. When the music stopped the leader would drop a broom stick between the closest couple, and they were the winner of the cake! It would be fun to win a cake I thought. Of course everyone went home with part of a cake but not the one they baked. Watching the couples laughing I wished my Mother could have been there. I really missed her and remembered her wonderful laugh that I loved so much. Everyone shared their cakes and we had coffee or other refreshments. A good time was had by all, even me.

All those cool mornings had finally led up to this, Thanksgiving Day was here. The long dining table had room for the whole family. We had a delicious and bountiful meal. It was provided mostly from Grandma's garden and her many days of canning. Our first

Thanksgiving at the farm was a wonderful and happy day.

The snow was coming down and Christmas would soon be here. It was time for our first Christmas program at school. All the parents and families would attend. The students put on a short program. It was really special to us because of the holiday season. After a big applause from the audience our treat was passed out. We all received a large bag of hard candy and a sweet orange. Thanks went to the women at the cake walk for their donations. School was out for two weeks during the Christmas holiday. It was the first time we would celebrate the birthday of Jesus at the farm. My sister and I received several lovely presents. Ronald was the one who was really excited about what was left under the tree for him. A Flexible Flyer was his present. Every boy wanted the fastest sled made, so he couldn't wait to use it. After breakfast was his chance! It only went half way down the hill. That was not far enough or fast enough for him. He begged me to jump on his back for added weight. Of course I foolishly did anything he asked. We flew down that hill until the sled hit a bare spot. My brother slipped forward and I landed on his head. His chin was buried deep in the snow. He was squirming trying to get me off him. He was yelling at me to get off his head at the top of his lungs. I paid no mind and was not very quick to what he demanded. It sure did make me feel good to get the best of Ronald for a change. It never happened very often but when it did I was sure proud of myself.

School started again and it was an uneventful winter. Walking to school those cold winter days was a great effort for me and the other students, but that was the way it was back in those days. We accepted all the hardships because we didn't know any different way. It

99

was good and happy memories with kids that were raised to be respectful and kind to each other. The only thing I knew and thought about often was that they were very lucky to have a loving mother to go home to every day.

Spring of nineteen twenty nine was lovely in the country. Golden forsythia was blooming. Apple, cherry, peach and pear trees had white, pink and yellow blossoms that soon would be fruit. After the last frost it was time for Grandma to plant this year's garden. She planted potatoes, cucumbers, tomatoes, peppers, and corn. There were many more vegetables too numerous to mention. We were really too young to help her much and she was very particular on how her seeds were planted. She wanted all the rows to be perfectly straight. I was sure I could not have done a good job. I stood back watching and wishing to myself that maybe next year I could help. Rhubarb came up every spring, and her rhubarb pies were the best in the country, or so I thought.

To my surprise Grandma asked me if I would like to go after her mail. I guess she really trusted me now that I was eleven years old. I felt very special. She cautioned me to not open any mail and not to look at her magazine. I think she had a few bad experiences with Ronald and Bob. They used to pick up the mail and opened it so they could not be trusted. Now maybe that was the reason she asked me. She didn't want us to view any of the pictures or read any of the stories in her "personal" magazine called *True Stories*. It was quite sexy for those times, so she was careful to keep it in her room for her own private enjoyment. I never did see one but knew they had to be something special. It was a long walk down the hill to the road, and before reaching the mailbox I heard someone calling my name. It was Sally my cousin, she was waving for me to come over to the barn. I knew it had to be

100

important and I was anxious to find out what she wanted to tell me. She quickly pulled me in the barn door and started whispering. I told her to speak up there was no one within miles. She talked real fast and told me her secret. ""You know the old man down the road who always wants to hug us and give us candy? He gave me some candy and then made me sit on the porch swing. He said he wanted to tell me where babies came from. He started talking about things I didn't want to hear about, especially from some old man." She said she thought he was up to something so she ran home. I was all ears but didn't learn much. I didn't know what to do or say. Everyone thought Elzy was a good old man. He had been the neighborhood miller at the county grain mill for years.

Nobody ever complained about his behavior that we knew about, but things like this weren't discussed in front of children. Sally and I decided we would never go to his house again. We were going to warn our younger sisters to never accept candy from him. Sally and I were special friends so we kept our secret. I went back home confused and puzzled. I though we should have told someone but being young girls without a mother we didn't know who to tell. I gave Grandma her magazine and mail. She laid the mail on the table and retired to her private quarters to read her ""True Story" magazine.

School would be over for the summer before we would know it. In May when summer vacation started the next holiday would be Decoration Day. This was the first time this was mentioned to us so we were puzzled. What was this all about? Many people in the country had a cemetery for their families. We never heard of such a thing in the city. The Lewis family was no exception we came to find out. The day before the holiday Grandma had picked beautiful flowers from her garden and yard. A large container full of water was put in the wagon. We placed the flowers in it gently so they would not wilt. The team of horses was harnessed to the big wagon. The horses knew where they were supposed to go when we crossed the road. Across the river they carried us in the wagon and waded slowly in the shallow water. Straight up the steep hill to the old homestead. We stopped there and had a basket lunch Grandma had prepared for the long ride. No one lived at the house then so it was our safe haven. Peanut butter sandwiches, rhubarb pie and cold tea never tasted so good. After our lunch break, forward and onward the horses led us to our cemetery at the end of the lane. There it was and for the first time I laid my eyes on the Lewis cemetery with head stones dating from the early 1800's. I thought that sure was many, many years ago. It was a beautiful place for all that were laid to rest there. My grandparents were very generous; I was told that any neighbors not having grave sites were welcome to rest in ours. Grandma and Aunt Belle handed each of us a flower to lie on each and every grave. All of us children were well behaved. We felt the respect Grandma and my Aunt showed while they carefully placed flowers on our loved ones graves. We were only there about a half hour and then we were ready to leave. I saw out of the corner of my eye the tears shed by my Aunt and Grandma as we loaded the wagon to head home. It was quite an experience, and one I have never forgotten. Before we had our evening meal we all bowed our heads in prayer and thanksgiving. I thought it was a wonderful day spend together in respect and love for our ancestors.

Early summer was a great time to catch lightening bugs. Of course we had to wait until it was dark to be able to get a glimpse of them. We were all sitting on the front porch after a hard day of work and chores. We were anxious to see the lightening bug party begin. I wondered where they stayed or nested in the daytime. I guessed no on knew so I sat quietly and did not ask. All the farm animals were bedded down for the night so you could hear a pin drop it was so quiet. Ronald, Bob, Francie and I had our glass jars ready for their arrival. Dad warned us to be very careful catching them because they are very fragile. He told us to get ready quickly; we would only have a half hour to get them into our jars. The lids had holes punched in them so the bugs could breathe, but not big enough to escape. It was now dark and they were beginning to come out floating in big bunches. I was ready in a flash but my brother and older cousin beat me to them by a hair. My cute little red headed sister was last. It seemed she could reach out and the bugs would fall into her hand. The hunt did not last long. Soon they scattered and went back where they came from. We all took our jars to show Dad. Each one was lit up like a candle. He got a big kick out of watching the hunt. Dad then looked at us and said, "You know you have to turn them all out in the fresh air or they will die!" We knew he was right so we reluctantly took the lids off and turned our jars upside down. All of us wished them well and good luck as we waved at them on their way. Thinking about this evening later I knew I would never forget those fun times and they would become fond memories.

Dad's original plan when we moved from Akron was to build a home for our family on the farm property. Grandma agreed the time had come for him to start the plans to build. He could have it ready before school started again he thought. Dad called his cousin that lived close by and asked if he would be available to help him build our house. He was willing to help so they started looking for building materials. The only choice they had was the deserted house across the river. It was the first house that our ancestors had built when they settled in West Virginia. It was originally a beautiful southern home they had raised their family in and had farmed the surrounding land. It was called the homestead and was still owned by Grandma. What a shame to have to demolish part of it for the lumber. The work was started and within a month all the lumber and supplies needed were transported to the location at the farm. Only windows, doors, and roof shingles would need to be bought by Dad.

Dad and his cousin Si pounded the last nail into the roof shingle. The both had worked hard to finish the house before school started. Now we were ready to move from Grandmother''s big house. Over in the meadow stood our new house, not too far, but just far enough. It seemed small to me at the time but we would make due. There were three rooms. In the middle was a door into the living room. It held two sitting chairs, a library table used for doing homework and a gas heating stove. On the left was a large bedroom that all four of us shared. There was a dresser that held all of our clean clothes. The kitchen had a basket that would hold our dirty clothes. A small gas cooking stove and a round table with four chairs was all that would fit in the small kitchen. A shelf was built especially to hold the dishes and kettles. We would have to heat water on the stove to wash our clothes and bathe. Some of the furniture had come from Akron. The dining table and chairs had been Mother''s pride and joy. We could not have left it behind. There was no electricity so we had an oil lamp for our light in the evening. Dad also built a necessary house. Almost every night my sister had to go outside to the privy. I always had to be the one to escort her and that lantern came in mighty handy. One great advantage was having free gas for cooking and firing up the big stove to heat the house in the winter. It was nice that Grandma had gas wells leased to the big oil companies. We three kids were now on our own as far as cooking, housekeeping and doing our own laundry. What a change for us, not being able to rely on Grandma. It was different but we were happy to be in our own little three room house. It didn't take us long to get settled into a routine with our chores. We missed Grandma''s home cooking, although we were invited to share her meals occasionally.

One thing Francie and I really loved was homemade cottage cheese. We knew Aunt Belle had churned a crock of it the day before and hadn't given us kids any of it. This day Grandma, Aunt Belle, and Bob went to the store in Cairo while Ronald and Dad were working in the corn field. Francie and I were looking around trying to figure out how we could get some of that cottage cheese while everyone was away. We went around Grandma's house to the dining room window; it was up pretty high and covered with a screen. We pulled a chair off the porch and stood on it so we could look in the window. I got a hammer and screw driver and we pulled that screen right off the sache and put up the window. Francie climbed up an over into the dining room and I followed right behind. There was a big dish of cottage cheese on the table. We each got a spoon and filled ourselves up with that delicious cottage cheese. While we had the chance we also ate some of Aunt Belle's other good food. We washed our spoons and put them back in place. It was getting late so we crawled back out the window, putting the screen back into place, moved the chair back onto the porch and went back to our little house with our belly's full. Of course we would never tell anyone what we had done. The next day Aunt Belle said "most of my cottage cheese was gone, do you two know anything about it?" We replied that we sure didn't know anything about it but we had our fingers crossed behind our backs. We stuck together in our fib and never ever told anyone about our cottage cheese escapade.

I really thought Grandma missed us a bit after we moved. She did have more time I guess to sew. I just knew she had to be missing us when she gave us a big surprise! It was on Saturday and I had been wishing I could have something new to wear to church. Grandmother called me over to the big farm house. She wanted to show me something real pretty she had made for me. In her hand she had something new and she told me it was mine. It was n new dress of purple and white stripes and it was just my size. She held it up against me and it was a perfect fit. A dream come true, I was so excited. She helped me try it on, how beautiful it was and I loved it. This is for church tomorrow she said. "Oh Grandmother, thank you so much, it is just what I needed to make me happy," I said hugging her tightly. The next morning I was so joyful. Grandmother had made Francie a dress also; everyone told us how pretty we looked. We skipped all the way home from church. After we had lunch, we played tag and hide and seek. I was crawling though the fence at the chicken roost and caught my new dress tearing a big strip out of the back skirting. I wanted to cry, why hadn't I changed into my play clothes? Oh me, oh my, how could I ever tell Grandmother? I was so upset and I knew she would be too. After thinking it over, I knew it was best to tell her right away. So here I went holding my dress tail in my hand, with tear dimmed eyes I found her on the porch. She knew right away something was wrong. I showed her my dress and she said, "I will fix it for you but it will never be as pretty as it was before it was torn."" I wonder who felt worse, me or my Grandmother. I learned a big lesson that day, I always changed my good clothes when I was supposed to and that Grandmother always knew best.

We did not get company very often. Dad's cousins from the city came to visit one day. They brought us a lovely house warming gift, a big beautiful Bible book. My sister and I memorized lots of the stories. It gave us much joy reading and learning from that book. It was quite a blessing when Francie won most of the contests at Sunday school. One of Dad's cousins played the violin so we all went over to Grandmother''s house. In the parlor Grandmother had a pump organ. I never could figure out why it was there because no one could play it. Since our older cousin had his violin we all begged him to play us a tune. He agreed and played several lovely songs. We were all impressed. When he invited one of us to try to play no one was interested in learning but me. When I told him I was left handed he said I would never be able to play the violin. What a disappointment! Grandma asked him if he would like to play her organ. He agreed and sat down and played it like an angel. I really thought I would love to take lessons. Grandma never wanted anyone in her parlor so organ lessons were out of the question.

Canning season was approaching, and President Herbert Hoover announced a sugar ration a year after being elected. It was 1930 and Grandma just had a few coupons to present to the store in order to be able to buy sugar. This was going to create a problem for her and many others who depended on canned food for the winter. She was forced to sell some of her bounty of peaches to the neighbors to save enough money to buy the sugar for this year. Drying fruit was one way of preserving it. Apples, peaches, pears and cherries were fine to dry, no canning needed. I helped attach the fruit to a screen, which was then attached to the back of the stove. The heat from the stove would allow the fruit to dry. The only other thing she could do when she ran out of sugar was use last years molasses. I heard her say the canned fruit would not taste as good or sweet but it must be done this year.

Summer was about over and it was almost time for school to begin. What an exciting time it had been the last few months, a brand new house and lot of adventures on the farm. Spending time with family and friends was special because it made it a little easier when my thoughts drifted back and I would miss my Mother. The first day at school all of us students had a big surprise; Mr. Moore was not the teacher sitting at the desk. A small woman not much taller than me stood there by the desk. She was greeting every student as we arrived. I thought to myself, what's going on? When we were all seated she introduced herself. "I'm Miss. McGregor; I'm your new teacher. Mr. Moore had to move away and is teaching at another school." I wondered at the time, how in the world this lady who weighed less than one hundred pounds could enforce the rules? In a few days we found out she had more regulations then Mr. Moore. She told us to follow them without any questions. She meant business but I came to like her a lot. The bigger boys either respected her or were intimidated by the stern look on her face most of the time. Those boys never caused any trouble.

Fall was here again for the second year in the country. Grandma's garden produced a tremendous crop. She shared all the vegetable, fruits and mutton meat with our family. Dad did not have enough time that year to plant a garden. No need, there was plenty and Grandma was very generous.

During the cool fall season some of the neighbors that raised sugar cane came on various days to make their molasses, they met at the school house yard. It was made near by so I would watch out the school windows with the other kids. They had a schedule of when each one would come and whose horse or mule would pull the wheel to turn the mill. The wheel turned and squeezed the cane until the juice came out into a bucket below. They had a big pot that was kept over a fire, and the juice was poured into the pot. It took a long time for it to boil and turn into molasses. It took barrels of cane to make one gallon of that thick substance. The family that brought the cane that day took that batch home. At times they would share with neighbors that did not raise cane. Any extra that wasn't needed would be sold.

Winter arrived with a lions roar. There was a chilling cold wind that blew straight through my clothes walking to school. No bus for the grade school kids so everyone had to walk. I felt sorry for my friends that had a much longer walk then me. There was hardly a time when a student missed a day because of the weather or sickness. We were a tough bunch! The first day of December on our way to school the snow started to fall. It was a beautiful sight, and it meant Christmas would soon be here. All of us kids could hardly wait for the holiday break. This would be the first year to celebrate Christmas in our own home. We knew we wouldn't get much, and the most we hoped for was the treat they passed out at church. Again our pastor ordered a large case of navel oranges from far away. He presented an orange to each church member. Sunday school teachers

109

filled small brown bags full of hard candy with a stick of cinnamon flavor. I was so glad we attended two different churches; it meant double treats for us!

We could hardly fall asleep as we anxiously waited for Christmas morning to arrive. Christmas Eve night Dad had laid out a bunch of grapes and a banana for Santa. They were two of his favorite fruits so he knew Santa would like them too. Next morning they were gone! We just knew Santa had stopped by; there were two small boxes under the tree. One was marked Marjerie and one marked Francis. We couldn't wait to open those boxes. I tried to guess what could be in such a tiny box. When we opened them we both squealed with delight. There was a ruby red ring for each of us. They were just what we had wanted, we couldn't have been happier. Dad was watching and broke out in a big smile. Christmas was always sad for him missing Mother, but he sure looked happy at that moment. It brought wonderful memories of Mother and I knew she would want us to be joyful and not sad. Ronald's gift was something he had also really wanted, another sled. Of course the one from last year hadn't lasted. He had wrapped it around a tree before winter was over. We all had a package of socks, underwear and a pair of gloves. Dad waited until we were all done opening our gifts. He was holding a package from us. We didn't have much money so Francie and I had gotten an idea. We remembered a box in the attic that had five beautiful old ties in it. We opened it, cleaned and pressed them to make his gift. When he opened them he was surprised and I thought pleased. He smiled at us showing off his gold tooth.

Grandmother, Aunt Belle and Bob came over to see us and brought unexpected gifts. Grandma gave each of us a scarf to wear under our coats. She knew we hardly ever fastened our coat buttons. I guess she was worried we would get cold walking to school. Aunt Belle made my sister and I each a nice dress. There was a new shirt and a sweater for my brother. Francie and I really liked our dresses and Ronald liked his new clothes. We three would have new outfits when we returned to school. My sister and I were also anxious to show off our beautiful new rings to every girl in school. We didn't want to brag but there was not one other girl that received a ring from their father for Christmas. It was a long hard winter but spring would be right around the corner.

Right before Easter Grandma had a phone call and it was bad news. Her sister Aunt Minnie had passed away that morning. She was told that a bad cold had turned into pneumonia and she hadn't survived. It happened right after my birthday of February 28th. This sad occasion brought back memories of my Mother going to Heaven so I knew how my cousins Sally and Evelyn Doris were feeling that day. My sister and I were not the only girls at school now without a mother. It put a lot of responsibility on Sally so I helped her when I could. She became my very best friend. Her sister and Francie became best girlfriends also. Uncle Lemon tried to get a housekeeper but it did not work out very well. From past experiences I didn't think too much of the idea.

Spring was here again and low and behold Grandma allowed me to help her plant her garden. Grandmother always wore a sun bonnet and lots of petticoats under her black skirt when gardening. She watched me as I was hoeing to ensure my rows were straight for her to plant her vegetables. I guessed at the time she must have thought I was a pretty good helper now that I was twelve. We had a really good time that day and I felt very grown up.

One afternoon Ronald, Bob, Francie and I were sitting around discussing the neighborhood news. We were in the living room and Dad was shaving in our little kitchen. The boys told us about a neighbor lady that had twins a few days prior. They said the twins could talk and walk right after they were born. We yelled at Dad and asked if this could be true? He yelled back and said he didn't know much about twins. With that reply the boys were encouraged to continue their tale. They can even read and write they told us. We were really anxious to go and see the twins and visit with their mother. We asked how soon we could go. Dad said with a grin that Mothers didn't feel too good for about a month so we would have to wait. The boys ran outside snickering and laughing. We found out soon after when we asked Grandma about these so called miracle twins. She looked at us and said, "The boys have fooled you two again." We learned not to believe everything they told us after that big lie.

School days were passing rapidly by. Maybe the reason was because I was older now and was used to our daily routine. School, church, chores and living in the country became the lifestyle that came natural to me. I still remembered living in the city but it was a distant memory now. My lovely Mother was the only memory that never escaped me. Living in our home was satisfying and happy times. Years went by extremely fast and before I knew it I was turning fourteen.

February 28, 1932 was my fourteenth birthday. It was our habit to paddle anyone on their birthday and give them a swat for each year. The biggest boy in school decided he was going to be the one to catch me and paddle me. I watched him real close and when he started to run after me I ran like a rabbit. Well, I ran out of the school yard and jumped a fence into a pasture, what a mistake! My feet landed in a fresh cow pile, soft, warm, and gooey. My dress flew up and my bottom went down right in that stinky pile. With tears in my eyes I said, "If you want to paddle me now is your chance." He just stood there and finally said, "I'm sorry, I will help you get up and walk you back to school." I was really a mess and headed straight to the girls outside toilet to try and clean up before recess was over. I asked Harry, "Would you have one of the girls bring some paper and a washcloth to me, I would really appreciate it?" ""Of course he answered" as he walked away looking real sorry for me. Now you know why I will never forget that special day on my fourteenth birthday.

The neighborhood Methodist church always had a revival in March. There were two ministers who held the meetings for two weeks each year. During this time the church asked the congregation for a member to volunteer to provide lodging for the two pastors. My Aunt Belle enjoyed cooking and having company so she volunteered for both of them to stay at the Lewis home with Grandmother's approval. When they arrived she graciously gave them the guest bedroom.

The revival started on a chilly Sunday evening. Everyone in the area attended as they always looked forward to this occasion each year. Our Aunt Belle took us three kids and her son Bob. The preacher that evening gave a message of salvation and how Jesus died on the cross to save us from our sins. I went to the altar holding my sister Francie's hand and we were both saved. Mrs. Delaney our neighbor was so anxious and excited, when she reached the altar she accidently fell on Francie. Her son came down and helped his mother up. Ronald and a few others were also saved that year. We all stood up front together for acceptance into the church membership and baptism. It was a glorious and successful revival. The last evening of the revival was on Saturday. The next day after Sunday church everyone gathered at the river for the baptismal service. While standing in the river waiting our turn, a big snake was swimming towards all of us. One of the men quickly went into the water and shooed the snake away. I remember how cold the river was when the three of us kids came up out of the water. Our family was Baptist and that is why we were immersed for baptism. My friend Cora Higgins and her family were Methodist and they were sprinkled with water. It was a good feeling to be saved and baptized. I thought now I could continue my life on the right path for the Lord. I was sure my Mother would have been pleased with me that day.

At the end of the school year, Miss. McGregor was still our teacher. I had become quite fond of her over the past few years. Many students went through the eighth grade and excelled under her teachings. It was finally my turn. There were four of us that had to take six tests to pass, arithmetic, history, geography, English, spelling and penmanship. Marjerie Pribble, Marion Simmons, Wayne Pribble and I arrived earlier than usual. The other kids had the day off so it was just us four and the teacher. Two tests were passed out at a time. I wasn't worried but I have to admit I was a little anxious. I was the first one to finish; we were allowed a short break so I went outside. Shortly Marion come out, he said he didn't think the tests were too hard. After lunch we finished all the subjects except for spelling. It was my best subject but one word stumped me, delicious. I had never seen that word before so I didn't even try to spell it. I knew I had passed but we would not get our grades for two weeks. A special letter came in the mail addressed to my Father and Mother. None of the teachers knew the three Lewis kids mother had gone to Heaven years ago. The letter was from the superintendent of the Richie county school system. Mr. Ramsey reported that I had done very well on my tests. He was proud to say I was eighth in the county with my high scores. I think my Dad was real proud too. It was a great day for me to graduate with honors. Graduation day had arrived; my good friends and I were thrilled. We had spent many years studying in a one room school house and it had paid off. There would always be lots of wonderful memories but now I was looking forward to attending the big brick school on top of that high hill. Cairo High School would be a challenge but I was ready.

During the summer the grass became scarce and Grandma had to move the sheep to another farm about two miles up the road. She would have to travel the main road to get there. What a magnificent sight it was seeing Grandmother riding side saddle on her beautiful horse Prince. To me she looked like a Princess with her Prince. I always wondered how she could stay on the horse, but she had been riding since she was a young child. The collie dog Spot was in the lead watching for strays. He would surround them and drive them back into the fold. What a smart dog he was and knew exactly what his duty involved. He was worth his weight in gold. If there was a car on the road they would move to the side and allow the sheep to pass. As soon as the sheep came to the turn off they turned right in and began moving faster many had been there the year before. They were fed and left in their enclosed pasture for the summer safe and sound. During summer if Grandmother disappeared we knew she Spot and Prince had gone to see about her sheep up in the holler. If Grandmother couldn't go up our one neighbor would check on them and report his findings to her.

That summer our church pastor asked me to teach one of the Sunday school classes. I accepted and it was a real pleasure teaching the younger children. The activities at the church took most of my time. I thought I would never endure the long summer months waiting for school to start.

It was September 1, 1932. Ronald, me and our cousin Bob would all start school at the same time this year. Little sister Francie had two more years in the one room school house. We three had to get up much earlier than last year because we had to catch a bus to school. The route went five miles to Cisco before it picked us up. When we saw it go by we had just enough time to run down the hill from the house to make it to our bus stop. This first day we were already waiting at the foot of the hill for the bus to arrive. Cousins Clarence, Carl and Sally lived close along the road and were always ready waiting on us. We were hoping the school bus driver had received the notice to pick up three new passengers. The big yellow bus was speeding down the road when he skidded to a stop. Wow!

There must have been twenty-five or thirty kids already on board. Where did all those kids come from I wondered? The bus driver was an expert at driving those crooked country back roads. The driver would let us out at the bottom of the school steps. I counted 100 steps to the top where the high school over looked the town. It was a beautiful sight from on top of the hill. As we looked out the top window of the school we could see down into the center of town and around the long road where the rest of the small town resided. What a wonderful place for a school.

I didn't have all the books I needed but I borrowed and did fine. I loved school and I especially loved English class. Three of us girls were very competitive with each other and very secretive about our grades. I listened as they told each other their grades, one had a 96%, and one had 95%. They seemed really happy with their grade till they asked what grade I received and I answered 98%.

I really didn't have much time at home as my sister and I did women's work helping out with farm chores. I did most of my lessons during school hours, getting good grades was very important to me. I was also studying Latin because I wanted to become a nurse. Most of my classmates had their mind on their sweethearts. I never had time to get acquainted with the city kids so I wasn't very well know in school. I did find out I really missed my sister; this was the first time we had been separated.

It was a cold foggy November morning for Election Day. It was raining and the roads were muddy with big ruts making it almost impossible to drive. Many people in the country did not have transportation to come to the voting poll at our school house in Rusk. At six that morning there were people lined up outside in the rain anxiously waiting for the poll to open. American flags were placed all up and down the road proudly marking the voting site. There were many people arriving on foot, men on horseback, and many buggies. Several men my Dad included drove back deep in the country side to pick up voters. More voters then you can imagine would unload out of one car. Each party would try and get as many voters to the polls so their candidate would win. Some of those people would only see folks every four years on Election Day.

The women enjoyed visiting and catching up on the community news. Showing off their new babies and a toddler or two no one had seen before. No alcoholic drinks were allowed in the school house or any other voting poll. Outside the men were laughing and talking of course about politics. It was quite some time before we actually knew who had won. Franklin D. Roosevelt a Democrat won that election and our family was sure he was going to make an outstanding President.

Another winter arrived in West Virginia with the roads being covered with snow and the trees were beautiful. To me the roofs and windows on the farmhouses looked like a white fairyland. I counted my blessing every day I rode to school. Walking was a thing of the past. Riding that yellow bus was certainly a bumpy ride but I wasn't complaining.

As I had said earlier my Grandmother was a shepherd of her sheep. She loved and took good care of them as they were her only income on the farm. She had each one named and they knew their names. Each morning she fed them grain and would call them by name and they would answer back. My Grandmother's name was Martha Cinderella Lewis and she was quickly recognized by the black clothing she always wore. She would wear a black bonnet, a long black skirt, black coat, and heavy galoshes. The sheep would see her coming and start running towards her bleating softly rubbing up against her walking stick. Spot would be in front of her guiding the sheep along keeping her from falling. She never got disturbed because I believe she knew those sheep loved her too.

It was spring 1933 and time was coming to sell the lambs. Lambing came in March and April while the snow was still on the ground. Each morning she would be up early and go count how many lambs had been born during the night. Little lambs are born with long tails, but in a short time they would be clipped. This prevented them from becoming covered with sheep droppings.

This was Grandma's spring income for the farm each year since Grandfather had passed away.

Today was an exciting day the lambs were to be weighed on the big scales. The lambs were lively, frolicking, and looked to be happy. They were so beautiful, white wool, black noses, and bobbed tails. They were led up to the scales without any trouble. After being weighed they were transported to the trucks that took them to be sold at the auction barn. Grandmother stood by watching, I noticed out the corner of my eye that she would wipe her eyes with her scarf. After all, these were her babies, and she loved her sheep dearly.

She would also earn money for the sale of the wool from her older sheep. This next event would be shearing of the wool which was a two man job. We loved to watch as one man would hold the sheep and the other one would shear the wool. The man with clipper would start at the head and finish at the rump. A heavy coat of wool came off which he would roll up into a bundle and tie it. The wool would be then be loaded onto a truck, weighed, and Grandmother would be given her check.

Grandmother rested only a day or so and then she got busy planting another huge garden. I was not very far away at our house when I saw her hard at work. For some reason I thought she looked tired and surely needed some help. She would not have asked me for help as we were living in our own home. She was such an independent woman. My sister and I hurried over and asked if we could help, I was happy she agreed.

Later that spring on an early cool foggy morning a sad accident occurred. My brother rose early and walked outside to see the fog rising in the meadow. Right below the fog he could barely see three horses and they were grazing where they did not belong. He called Dad and said he would scare them back to the other field with his rifle. By that time Francie and I were up from all the commotion. We were watching their every move and heard Dad tell Ronald that he would do it because he was a better shot. He aimed for the meadow and pulled the trigger. In a moments time one of the horses reared its head and started to run. Dad dropped the rifle and yelled, "I have killed Maws riding horse Prince! What am I going to do, she will never forgive me." Dad and Ronald took off at a run. Out to the meadow and down over the hill as fast as they could run. They told us they found beautiful Prince lying on his back with legs straight in the air. Dad knew immediately the horse was dead. They both walked slowly towards our house. Dad looked totally devastated with grief. We would never dare tell what happened. Grandma would not know unless Dad told her himself. I watched as Dad walked through the gate to the big house. His sisters met him at the door and knew something bad had happened. They stopped him on the porch and asked what was wrong. He told them, "I accidently shot Maw's horse and I have to tell her." They could not believe what they heard him say. They thought, not Prince, this is such a tragedy. They told him to wait and think it over before telling her this horrible news. After a short while he was better composed and decided he must tell her right then. She was grief stricken and began sobbing. Later that morning I saw them walking out to the meadow and Dad was holding her hand. Dad said she had asked him if the two boys and he would bury Prince properly. Of course he agreed. Grandma appeared heartbroken as she walked back to her big house very slowly. We really missed Prince because we had always seen him each day grazing peacefully in the field. I will never forget that sad, sad day for all the family.

Summer was slowly cooling down and crops would soon be put up for the long winter months that would surely be here soon. A lot of work needed to be done in a short period of time. The garden did not produce as much as past years so it would be hard to feed the whole family. It was time for Grandmother to go down the road on foot and herd her sheep back to the pasture at the farm. Later they would be safe from the winter storms in her barn. It had not been a good year for Grandma and profits from the sheep were low. She knew by the end of summer she would not be able to pay Dad any longer for his hard labor. After six years at the farm she had no choice but to tell Dad she could not afford him, she was almost out of money. I'm sure it must have been a very difficult decision. I always thought that possibly this decision was partly because of Prince, I was never sure. Dad was desperate trying to find work. One of the neighbors that had just returned from Ohio knew he was looking for a job and gave him a lead. He said he knew a farmer that was paying $25.00 a month for farm help. He told Dad that it was a nice place to live. He left out the part about how hard the work was and the many hours a day that was involved. After Dad wrote the farmer and was hired, it was settled we would move to Johnstown. We three kids had no choice in the matter. At the end of summer before school started we were on our way headed north to Ohio.

Chapter Five
Moving to Johnston

DAD REALLY THOUGHT THIS WAS THE RIGHT thing to do and would have a good job to support his family. If he had been told the truth about the situation I don't think he would have considered moving. Now we were all committed for a whole year. In spite of poor directions we finally found the place. What a disappointment when we drove up the dirt driveway. A big old dark, gloomy and spooky house. We were all tired from traveling from West Virginia to Ohio in only one day. After finding the two beds we collapsed and fell asleep. The next day we found out what we didn't want to know. We were in more trouble then we thought. No electricity, no inside plumbing, no running water, no rugs on the floor and only coal lamps for light. In the kitchen was a coal cook stove and an ancient table and four chairs. In the so called living room was a big coal heater for the up coming winter months. On the other side of the room was a library table and two dirty sitting chairs. At that point we sure did not know what the future would bring. I thought to myself and then said to my siblings, "How can we live in this place for a year?" Father's chores starting the first day was to milk the cows, feed the pigs and chickens before breakfast. We three wandered outside. There was not a house close by and a very long drive to the main road.

It was getting near time for school to start. We found out that Francie would go to the village school close by. Ronald and I would be enrolled at Johnstown high school.

It was located about two miles away and there wasn't any school buses in that town. We would have to walk and I was not thrilled about those conditions. We had lived in rural West Virginia but we at least had school buses for the high school students. I thought what kind of town is this? It wouldn't be long now before we would have to prepare for the first day of school in this strange town, and I dreaded the thought.

Right after we moved we had a surprise visitor. Uncle Floyd Null came to stay with us. He was my mother's older brother. That was the way things were in those days. Family members would visit without asking, and most of the time they were welcome. Every day he went into town and did not return until supper time. After staying for a couple of weeks another guest arrived. It sure was a surprise to us when he appeared with his girl friend. We all got along well. My sister was real pleased because we knew her back home and had liked her. She was a good cook and helped us with the house cleaning.

One evening while sitting on the seat of the outside toilet gossiping, a funny thing happened. We saw several of the chickens staggering around. She said they looked like they were drunk. Curious me, went over to inspect the corn they had been eating. It was all mashed up and smelled potent. I said," I think there is something going on here we do not know about!" She never said a word. I always wondered what made those chickens act so silly.

It wasn't long after that, father had a talk with them. He told them they would have to find another place to live. There was not enough money to support us and them too. After my uncle had found a job at the local pharmacy they left. They rented a house close to the high school. My sister and I missed her very much. It was almost like having a mother figure living with us. When she left it made me think about mom and I missed her even more.

After I started to school I spilled chocolate milk all the way down my dress, and immediately thought of her so I ran to her house. She was ironing but when she saw what a pickle I was in she stopped everything. She helped me get my soiled dress off and washed it. I almost cried. She consoled me and said, "Everything will be just fine, don't worry." She then pressed my dress until it was dry. After I put it back on I kissed and hugged her. I never told her how much I loved her. Her name was Beatrice.

High school was not exciting at all. Compared with our hometown high school in Cairo, West Virginia, it was awful. I missed all my friends and wonderful teachers. I endured it because I had no choice. Fall arrived in Ohio.

My sister and I decided to pay a visit to our land lord's family. She knew the children from school. It wasn't far to walk that chilly Saturday morning. Their mother opened the door, and Francie told her who we were. She had never met us before. The kids were happy to see us, a ten year old boy and his sister eight. We were all having a good time when we heard their parents quarreling. He had asked her to sew some buttons on his trousers. She then replied that she would absolutely not do it. I don't know why I spoke up and said, "I know how to sew buttons." At the time I didn't think it was rude to offer. It was my mistake to speak up like that because I was taught to be quiet and I always did what father said. No one said a word until he spoke up and agreed for me to do the job.

He gave me a pair of his trousers with suspenders and showed me where to sew the buttons. This took the rest of the evening. It was getting late so we left for home, and when we arrived the house was dark. We were trying to be quiet, but when I thought I had found a chair to sit in I flopped to the floor with a bang. Ronald and dad woke up and demanded to know where we had been all evening. After explaining, we were so glad to get to bed. The next morning the land lord stopped by. This was a rare occasion. He thanked me for sewing the buttons on his pants. He hesitated and said, "" the only problem you sewed them on upside down but I did get my suspenders fastened." I thought to myself it was better then letting them fall down in public. My sister and I went in the house as fast as we could. We looked at each other and had a big laugh.

There were a few good times that fall. The school took us on a field trip to the next county where maple syrup was made. The maple tree juice was caught in buckets attached to the side of the tree. The liquid was picked up, then poured into bigger buckets. The big buckets were delivered and poured into huge cooking containers. They were placed on a wood fire pit. It took many hours to boil the liquid down to finally become syrup. The aroma of maple syrup filled the air for miles. We were glad dad came with us that day. He broke down and bought a quart to take home. The next morning we filled our bellies with pancakes smothered in fresh made butter and delicious maple syrup.

Winter had arrived. It was cold and snowing most days when my brother and I had to walk to high school. Two miles didn't sound too far until we started walking. We hurried down the long stretch of that windy highway.

There wasn't much traffic. Soon a car load of boys Ronald got acquainted with at school squelched to a stop. They picked him up and left me standing by myself on the highway. I should have told my father but I learned early not to tattle on my brother. Another thing that I found out about him was he told everyone his name was Oscar. I never knew if he ever told them the truth. Just one time I was offered a ride home. A young student I didn't know stopped with a car full of girls. He told me I could ride but the only room was on the running board. It beat walking so I jumped on holding on for dear life. I stepped down off the car before it stopped. I fell backwards landing on my back, stunned but not hurt. I never accepted another car ride.

December of 1933 was probably the loneliest and sadist Christmas because I don't remember much about it. I don't think we even had a tree and only a few little gifts. It was not like our wonderful holidays in West Virginia. I was homesick for the family.

Spring of 1934 eventually was here. One afternoon when dad came home for lunch, Francie and I asked him if we could go back with him. We wanted to look around the barn where he worked. He said he would be very busy and to stay out of his way. Good thing he cautioned us to look before we stepped. We remembered this from farm life experience and being around cows so we were mighty careful. Milking time was near and Dad herded the cows in their stalls. He started milking one at a time. Almost every cow had a calf and they were hungry. They all ran around with their tails twisted and mouths open. What a racket it was, bawling of calves and cows all at once.

Dad finished milking all ten of the cows. He then had to fill the big milk cans and close them. Selling milk was one of the profits for the farmer. Each calf ran to it's mommy but if it wasn't the right one it was butted away. It was fun to watch.

After a cold and long winter I was enjoying the spring weather despite being very melancholy. I was trying my best not to think of grandma working in her garden and many other memories of spring on the farm. It didn't work! I was still missing her and Aunt Belle so much I could hardly stand it. I cried myself to sleep many nights thinking about them and the rest of my family in West Virginia. I had visions of grandmother riding side saddle on Prince all dressed up in a black bonnet, black blouse and a black skirt with all those crinolines under it. What a beautiful sight, even if it was only in my dreams. Missing my aunt that was always so good to us and made the best cottage cheese in the world made me sad. Longing to be back where I belonged in West Virginia. Time passed and I survived.

Ronald was always in the woods exploring or I should say looking for trouble. While roaming around he spied a mother groundhog. She was taking her babies out of their hole in the ground to sun themselves. I will never know how he caught all four of them. He brought them back home for Francie to feed. She was so good with animals. We fed each one with a spoon full of milk. It took a long time but it was loads of fun. We gave three of them away. When we were finally down to one, we named him Bobby. Dad must have liked him and thought we needed a pet. He was so cute and smart. When he heard us eating at meal time he climbed up on the porch. He then would bump his nose on the screen door until one of us would jump up and let him inside. My sister would make him beg for a piece of cornbread. He stood up on his hind legs and begged just like a dog. We would laugh and laugh. He would eat anything we did. Early one morning I went into the pantry to get a crock of milk for our breakfast. There was Bobby standing on his hind legs, his front foot in the crock with his face all covered with cream. His eyes bugged out with fright when I yelled, "Bobby what are you doing?" After licking his paws he jumped down and ran as fast as his little legs would carry him. Out the door he went. He knew he had done something wrong. From then on I always checked each night that the pantry door was tightly fastened. He had a warm bed in the coal bin where he stayed at night. He was an unusual kind of pet but we cherished him. He loved to ride in the car with us and we never left him behind.

It was a very exciting day. We found out dad was told he could have a little time off. It was a slow time at the farm. The landlord could handle all the chores himself for a few days. We didn't have to be told twice to pack our suitcase. We were going to grandma's for a short visit. We were ready in a flash including Bobby in the back seat. Our old Model T was headed south. While stopping for gas, the filling station owner wanted to buy Bobby. Of course we told him we would not part with him for any price. Visiting grandma and the rest of the family was a thrill. My grandma Null and cousins, Rhoda and Monelle were surprised and delighted to see us. We were there on a Sunday so of course we went to church and saw many of our friends. They were all happy to see us and said they missed us. All our cousins and friends dearly loved Bobby. He was quite an attraction. They played with him like a kitten. We put him in the cellar house one day when we went away. When we returned we couldn't find him anywhere. Everyone looked and looked but he was no where to be found. We imagined he squeezed out somehow searching for us. What a great loss. We should have taken him with us!

Aunt Grace, mother''s younger sister, gathered some clothes for us to take back. I was told she adored my mom. She always was so generous and kind to us. A week passed fast and then it was time to start back to Ohio. I dreaded the thought especially without Bobby. He was the most joy my sister and I had that whole miserable year. When we arrived back at Johnstown my unhappy life started all over again in that strange place.

Dad bought a jersey cow shortly after we got back. We named her Mazie. He came from the barn one evening after milking, quite upset. He told me that his prize winning cow was not giving her regular amount of milk. He knew there was a problem and had to get to the bottom of it. He didn't think she was sick but wanted me to keep a close eye on her. I promised I would watch her closely. He said that she just stands and flips her tail and looks at him with her big brown eyes. There is something she is doing she doesn't want us to know about. He asked me if I would want the job of detective. How pleased I was, being chosen by dad to be his detective. I would have to watch and spy like a real live story book sleuth. I took the job seriously and I was going to be ever alert. She never suspected anything out of the ordinary because she didn't pay any attention when I was around. She loved me and I her. The next morning after milking the cows were turned out to pasture. About noon I saw her go behind the barn. Just then a piglet ran down the path to the barn. He was squealing loud and running fast. The last three days he had done the same thing. I became suspicious and decided to slip up behind him quietly and see what he was up to. Well, what do you know I found out all right. Mazie was swishing her tail to keep the flies off her back. That's not all I saw, that piglet was climbing up her hind leg reaching and stretching for the cow's tit. Milk was running down both sides of his jaws as he was sucking. He must have thought he was in hog Heaven!

Mazie was just standing real still chewing her cud. She looked at me as if to imply she was just feeding this hungry little baby. Now I knew where all that milk was going. I watched the pig run back to the pig pen. He went straight to a hole in the fence and slid through. Now I knew both of their secrets. When I made my report to dad he laughed hysterically. Who would have dreamed of such a situation? He was pleased at my detective work and so was the landlord. I felt like the only problem with this true story was that I didn't get paid for my excellent detective work. I was determined to never work for free again. That evening when father was milking Mazie I heard him whisper in her ear, ""You think you were the sly one feeding that piglet don't you? Tomorrow the fence will be mended and he will not be able to meet you behind the barn ever again. Your good deed is over." She kept on chewing her cud, looking innocent as always. Then she threw back her head, as if to understand everything dad had said. With a loud moo I imagined she was trying to tell us, "Too bad my secret is not my secret anymore but it was fun while it lasted."

My heart seemed to be almost breaking at times. That old house was so dreary and disappointing. I was so lonely. No where to go, no one to talk to and not knowing what to do about it. Not even a telephone to call grandma. We had not received a letter from grandmother since we came home from our short visit. I was very lonely and could not tell anyone how horribly I missed my mother. I felt all alone. I believe dad began to see we were all three quite unhappy. He gave us the good news. We were not staying another year. We were ecstatic to think of going back to our home in West Virginia. Back to our family and friends. Back to the little church I loved so well. I knew Francie needed someone to make over her again. I loved my little sister but I couldn't replace the love she felt when grandma and Aunt Belle would hug and kiss her.

She said she wanted to look real pretty the last day at school. We didn't know much about sewing but we had an idea. Our mother's "White" pedal sewing machine was in the attic. In the dresser we found a new piece of brown and red flowered material. It was just large enough for a dress. There was still a dress pattern for Francie in the drawer. We cut it out and I started to sew. We had a lot of fun doing our best, taking turns sewing. I trimmed it with red rick rack. When it was finished she tried it on for size. There was something wrong. I had sewed the sleeves on backwards. What a laugh we had. It took some time to re-do the sleeves but the dress turned out nice. She looked so cute with her long strawberry red hair. She was very pleased because she had a new dress to wear her last day at school. We became extremely bonded that year. I don't know how we would have survived without each other. I thanked God many times for giving me a sister like Francie. School was dismissed for the summer at Johnstown. It was not a sad occasion for me. I had not made any true friends that year. I was glad to leave and couldn't wait to pack and get things ready for our move back home to West Virginia. Father had written to grandmother to confirm our return. I really didn't want dad to know how I felt about this past year. He tried to be mother and father to us kids. I knew he was doing the best he could.

We were anxiously awaiting for the moving truck to arrive. Outside we stood staring down the road. We were so glad when we saw a glimpse of Uncle Bernard's old truck. He slowly drove down the long, dusty driveway. What a big surprise! Bob jumped out of the truck and ran towards Ronald. They were jumping up and down embracing. What a sight! I guessed they missed each other more then I thought. They were buddies, always getting into trouble on the farm. Arguing a lot just like brothers even though they did not look alike. Ronald had rusty, red hair and brown eyes. Bob was blonde and blue eyed but they couldn't have been more alike. Both boys were eighteen and were a lot of help. Loading the truck did not take much time. We had not brought many possessions. Fresh water was one thing we did not forget. Uncle Bernard reminded us several times for a good reason. The last passenger to load was Mazie, our prize winning jersey cow. We certainly couldn't leave her behind. We were on our way. Ronald and Bob riding with my uncle in the truck, Francie and I in the front seat of the car with dad. Down the road we went for the last time and I could not have been more pleased. This day was the happiest moving day for everyone. Although I think I was the happiest of all. Ohio was behind us.

It took only about six hours to arrive at the farm. The dogs greeted us with excitement, jumping all over us. They sure have not forgotten us I thought. Grandmother and Aunt Belle were waiting in the front yard. They heard that old moving truck start up the hill at the road. How wonderful to be hugged and kissed again by family that missed us and loved us as much as they did. Before anything else was unloaded dad showed off our beautiful cow to everyone. He tied a rope around her neck and she walked close to him down to the barn. She behaved really good on the trip. I think she knew she was going to her real home now. That gentle jersey cow was a part of our family. The truck was unloaded. Some furniture and personal items were left in the front yard so our uncle could return to his home after a long day driving. What would we have done without him? He was always ready to help. What a blessing to be back home with our beloved family. I now had the satisfaction of feeling safe again and not all alone.

Quite a surprise was in store for us when we ventured over to our little house. We were intending to move our things right back in but that didn't happen. Dad's sister Aunt Ellen, answered the door with her three children. Dad was speechless. Grandmother had not warned him about this little problem. I guess, to begin with they had assumed we would never come back. Disappointment could not describe the feeling we all felt at that moment. Of course he couldn't ask his sister to move. When we returned to the farm house we were ready for a good meal. It tasted delicious. One of the things I had missed was grandma's cooking.

Grandmother then directed Francie and I to a bedroom upstairs. As we climbed the twisted stairway we were holding our breath. She told us to carry our traveling bags to the first room at the top of the stairs. We were so excited. It was the room we had really hoped for. It was small with a big Texas star painted on the ceiling. She glided past the room then turned back and said, "This was your Uncle Dallas's room. He painted that star on the ceiling after he graduated from college in Plano, Texas. He would be happy to know his niece's will be enjoying it now." We threw our arms around her and told her that this room was the answer to our dreams. As she walked down the steps she said she hoped we would be happy and she loved us very much. How wonderful to be home in West Virginia again.

The next day we had to face the major situation that had developed. It was a unexpected challenge for our family.

Dad had to find us a place to live.

Chapter Six
Summer Time 1934

WHEN GRANDMOTHER INVITED US TO STAY with her until we could find a home, we were relieved. In a few days dad started driving around looking for an empty house. He found out that when one family moved out another one would immediately move in. It was pretty discouraging. He asked all the neighbors to let him know right away if they knew of anything for rent. Even the minister inquired on Sunday from the pulpit. None of the congregation was aware of any house available. He had no choice but to keep trying and hope for the best. Grandma always made us feel welcome. We felt fortunate our family was supportive in our time of need.

I became accustomed again to the way of life at the farm. It wasn't very hard because I was again happy. Now I could use the telephone to call my cousins. Before this, children was not allowed to use the phone. I guess the women were afraid we would be able to listen to all the news. Some was good news and some bad but mostly neighborhood gossip on the party line. There were no numbers to dial just a short or long ring when you turned the handle. I finally reached my grandma Null's telephone after many a try. I was told it was O.K. to visit the next day.

Dad drove down that familiar bumpy road to the small settlement of Gallaspi where they had always lived. We did not get to spend much time with them when we had visited in the spring. My grandparents were known as

134

mommie and poppie. Hugging and kissing was one of the traits we loved about them. Rhoda and Monelle met us in the driveway before the car came to a stop. Dad went into the house to discuss all the things that men talk about with grandpa. Our two cousins were beautiful young girls. They resembled the Lewis side of the family with their dark hair. Francie and I looked more like the Null's with our red hair. My sister had long strawberry red, curly hair. Mine was straight as an arrow and fiery red just like my mother's. The rumor around the country side was, we four were the prettiest girls for miles. We seemed to attract a lot of attention when we were together especially from the teenage boys. After we were there a while we decided to sit in the Model T and tell secrets like girls do. I never knew why, but somehow that car started. Rhoda reached over and pulled the gas lever down and away we went. I was the lucky one in the driver's seat. We were going really fast bouncing over the rough country road. It was muddy with deep tire ruts. If the car had not stayed on the road and slipped into those ruts we would have been stuck like glue and in big trouble. My cousin reached over again and pulled the lever down all the way. Francie and Monelle were in the back seat jumping up and down screaming stop, stop! I was having a hard time steering and trying to keep the car on the road. Rhoda thought it was funny! I yelled real loud for her to turn the gas lever up so the car would stop. Finally she must have realized we were in danger so she did what I demanded. The car then slowed down enough for me to turn it around in a wide spot in the road. We were then slowly headed back towards the farm.

The old folks were standing in the middle of the road waiting for us. They had heard the loud screaming and came outside to see what was happening. When they realized the car was gone and so were we, grandma started crying and almost fainted according to Dad. I stopped the car right in front of them. I was glad I stopped it before running down over the hill into the creek. Dad and grandpa were quite upset with us. We scurried out of the car and ran like scared rabbits to the house. We were scolded and were told we had to stay inside all day. Grandmother read Bible stories to us. She wanted to teach us how wrong it was to disobey. My sister and I thought we got off easy. Although we were still a bit scared of what dad would say or do after we left. He never said much in front of our grandparents. We were reprimanded and lectured all the way home that evening. As soon as we went in the back door nothing more was ever mentioned.

Grandmother Lewis asked me again to start picking up her mail at the bottom of hill. I guess she was getting a little older. All that way down and back every day was a long walk, but she would have never admitted it. I was glad to help her in any way I could. True Stories magazine was still coming in the mail and I delivered it straight to her as before. She retired to her room with the magazine.

It was the first of June. Dad drove around again asking about rentals again. He went a little further away then before. No luck! Looked like it was going to be some time before we could move.

Grandmother was getting low on her supply of soap. It was time to make her homemade lye soap for the year. It was her special recipe and her secret. Soap making was a mystery to my sister and I. We were curious to learn. In past years we were too small to help and she never allowed children to be around when she brewed her soap. It was a hot job and a bit dangerous, especially for little ones. Homemade soap was used for washing clothes, dishes, scrubbing floors, Saturday night bathes and shampooing our hair. Lye soap made our red hair glisten and shine. My brother always had poison ivy or dew sores on his feet. She heated the soap and mixed in a small amount of sulfur and the problem was solved. She was part Indian, making her an expert on homemade medications and old time healing treatments. The boys brought the large iron pot out of the cellar. We knew this was the day grandma was going to make the lye soap. Francie and I were old enough now so we volunteered to help build a fire. We begged grandma to let us learn how to make soap. She thought for a minute, then told us if we were very, very careful we could help. We three carried the heavy iron pot and put it on the three legged stand over the fire. She poured water and lye into the pot first. Next bacon grease, pork grease, beef grease and sheep tallow were added. These ingredients had been saved back and stored for the future soap mixture. She said," I will stir for awhile until it blends because I don"t want either of you to be burned by the lye." She was right! A dangerous job it was when it started to boil and the soap bubbled and popped. In a while she turned the stirring over to me. The wooden paddle had holes bored in it so it would be easier to stir the thick solution. Grandma left to do her morning chores, trusting we would be O.K. My sister came close and took a whiff. She snorted, "Pee you! This stuff sure stinks. Do you think we can spice it up a little ?" I asked her if she meant cinnamon or cloves but she thought a liquid would work better. Only one thing left we could think of was vanilla. She whispered, "Vanilla would be a great idea, maybe I could slip by grandma and get her big bottle of Watkins vanilla without her seeing me?" I told her to try. She sneaked quickly around the tool shed and into the house. Soon she came back and said, "Now you do your part." I opened the big bottle and starting pouring, being careful to not use it all. My sister had told me not to use it all because grandma may need some. I thought maybe she would not notice that most of it was gone if I did what Francie suggested. Never a good idea to try to deceive. We knew this was true but did it anyways. As I handed her the bottle back, here came grandma around the corner of the house. Sister quickly hid the bottle under her apron.

"How is everything going? That's strange, something sure smells like vanilla," she said looking straight at us. We never said a word. Grandma looked puzzled then shook her head when she started stirring again. The soap was soon done to her satisfaction and she let it cool. Later that evening she dipped the soft mixture into a long, flat metal pan. The next day she cut it into bars. "Well girls I know why this the soap has the aroma of vanilla. I discovered my Watkins bottle almost empty. I think this batch smells a lot better then any other I have made,'" she said with a grin. Boy were we delighted. We should have known she was way to clever and observant for us to fool.

June was when the local boys and girls baseball teams were organized. The teams were named Petroleum One and Petroleum Two. Girls were included so we would have enough players for both teams. Some of the girls even played better then the boys. It was our turn to have the game at our farm. We rotated each Sunday to different location. The game started with a bang. A young boy hit a home run. The ball hit the bat with a loud crack. He ran like lightening all the way to home base. Everyone clapped and shouted, " Way to go number 1," as he slid into the base. When he got up we all saw the whole back of his pants had split out. Aunt Belle was fast to run over and cover him up with her apron then escorted him to the house. She gave him an pair of Bob's trousers to wear. Quickly she pulled out the old pedal sewing machine and in a jiffy sewed his pants up like brand new. He put them back on and strutted outside as a hero. We only had three balls so we would lose at least one a game in the meadows. Which ever team won was not important. It was a lot of fun and exercise. Aunt Belle served cookies and her famous lemonade to both teams. Late in the afternoon the gang left walking and some rode their horses. Most of us met at church later. Of course we had to decide which farm to meet at the next Sunday. That would be another exciting day for all who played and attended.

Once in a while grandmother would disappear. Most of the time we knew where she had gone. When her grain bag was missing we knew she was taking sweet grain to her sheep. It was just plain grain but she put a drip of molasses in it as a special treat. She carried a full bag over her shoulder walking through the meadow to the barn.

A walking stick and Spot was her only safety. She was so faithful caring for her flock. The sheep always knew her voice and came running when she called. One day she was gone way too long. Aunt Belle was getting worried so she asked my brother to go and see what was wrong. The sheep barn was about a quarter of a mile away. When he heard Spot barking he started running. He saw her black robe on the ground and heard her yelling. Grandmother told him she had slipped and fell. She couldn't get up or put any weight on her foot and her ankle was swollen by that time. Ronald was a big young man. He lifted her up in his arms gently. He started walking towards the house slowly then put her down so he could run to call for my aunt for help. When Aunt Belle heard him yelling she went quickly to her mother's rescue. He carried grandmother into the living room and laid her on the divan. She was in a lot of pain and Dr.

Douglas was called to come as soon as possible. He was much respected and knew everyone in the district. He knew how to come to the Lewis farm but it still took him about a hour. Arriving in his Model T as soon as he could with just a few medical supplies he rushed to her side. The only thing he could do was to wrap her broken ankle joint and put splints around it. Grandma was on crutches for a long time and could not walk well enough to go out of the house. My sister and I tried to help her all we could by carrying meals to her room. She was extremely independent and never asked for anything unless it was necessary. We found out how many chores and the enormous responsibility she had every day. We did our best to help and was happy to do anything she asked.

My other aunt that was staying in the house dad had built had a daughter and two boys. Our cousin''s Charles and Denver liked to play in the bigger barn that had a silo. All the hay, corn and feed were stored in there to feed the animals in the winter. Suddenly we heard the boys screaming," FIRE, FIRE! " Aunt Belle and I grabbed two big buckets and ran for the barn. She pumped water from the cistern to fill the buckets. We poured water on the fiery cornstalks, but of no avail. Too, too late the fire kept running and growing bigger and higher by the second. It jumped into the hay in the silo. I screamed, " Let's go to the back of the barn before the fire reaches it and try and salvage what we can.''" We saved some saddles, harness's and tools. Because the fire was so tremendously hot that was all we could save. Someone at the house rang the dinner bell furiously for help. That was the message everyone in the country knew when a family was in trouble. Sadly the neighbors were too far to hear it but it was too late anyways. Grandmother was in the house frantically staring out the window. She was still on crutches and almost collapsed. I thought she must have felt so helpless. She looked as if her world had come to an end. My heart was broken to see my grandmother so devastated. One thing we were thankful for was it happened in the middle of the day. All the animals were out of the barns and in the fields. It took a long time before grandma fully realized the barn had burned to the ground. We wondered how those boys got the matches out of the tin box way up on the kitchen wall. My cousins were very sorry and told grandmother they didn't mean to set the barn on fire, they were only playing. Late that afternoon father and my brother came in from working on the farm across the river. They couldn't believe their eyes. Unfortunately they didn't hear the dinner bell or see the fire from where they were working. They smelled the smoke but thought a farmer near by was burning brush. The horses and cows were turned loose in the fields after that tragedy. They had no barn to rest and bed down at night. A new barn was built before winter but not as big and grand as I thought the original one was. We all regretted what had happened but had to accept the things we couldn't control. During those days, back in the country that was just the way it had to be. There was no way to change what was in the past.

After many months of searching for a house so our family could move, dad was at his wits end. There was nothing available, absolutely nothing. Finally grandma and him came up with an idea. He explained to us this will be the last resort.

Chapter Seven
Moving to the Old Homestead

AFTER TELLING US WHAT THEIR PLANS were, dad and grandmother drove over to the old homestead. The road was so rocky they had to walk part of the way up the hill.

It had been deserted for some time. They didn't know if it was still livable. Looking over the place took them most of the day. One important thing about a house that's been standing empty for a long time, is a possible leaking roof. It was a miracle that the old tin roof was still in good shape. The windows and doors were also in decent condition. They thought it would need improvements and a lot of work but there was no other choice. Dad's mind was made up, he had found a place for us to live.

The history of that old house goes way back in time. It had been built in 1885 by my great grandparents. Several of their boys moved to Texas. They fell in love with the great state of Texas and raised their families there and never returned to West Virginia. The old folks finished their days living in their home here. My grandparents went to Texas and tried it for a few years. They returned and built the big house on the opposite hill where grandma still abides. From time to time family members have lived in the original Lewis homestead and now it would be our turn.

Dad and grandma made a schedule for the work days.

Ronald, Bob, family and friends agreed to help with the undertaking. Grandmother gathered all the cleaning supplies we would need. The wagon was loaded and we started across the river to the old house.

All the floors had been replaced by the men ahead of our trip. A few of the window glass had to be replaced. Now it was time for the women to take over inside. Grandma, Aunt Belle, Francie and I teamed up to get the work done faster. We scrubbed and cleaned all the rooms. Washed the windows with vinegar to make them shine. The house was not perfect but it looked spic and span to us when we finished. The men worked outside building a barn for Mazie. The outhouse was built, no inside plumbing! The road had to be repaired so dad could drive the Model T clear up to the house. It took a lot more work then we all anticipated, but it was now ready for us to move in.

The day before we moved most of our clothes were already packed in boxes. Of course this final move as teenagers would be complete if only my mother was still here. I was still missing her lovely smile most every day. I hardly slept a wink that very last night in the Texas star bedroom. When the dawn peeked over the horizon my sister and I jumped out of bed and away we went to meet the new day. It was a great and exciting morning for our family, grandma included, I'm sure. The wagon was loaded with two beds, two living room chairs and a library table we had kept from the other house. My mother's dining table and four chairs that meant so much to us were tied on the back, and finally the horses were ready to trot. It was late August 1934 when we started down the Lewis farm hill, over the road, then crossing the river at the ford. We had lived with grandma again for about three months. The team pulled the heavy load up the steep hill to our new home. The men were waiting to help unload the wagon when we arrived.

It didn't take them much time to take the furniture into the house. One bed was set up in the living room for dad and Ronald. The other one was carried up the narrow steps to a small bedroom for Francie and I. There was a straw tick mattress. You can imagine, it was not very comfortable. A small dresser grandma gave us was the only other furniture in our room. Just a few hangers on a rope was the closest thing to a closet we had. Now it was starting to look like a home to me. When we went back down those windy steps to the kitchen, there it was! Right before we moved dad searched for a stove. I thought it was a poor excuse after examining it. No oven to bake bread and in very bad shape. My sister and I just stared at each other. We knew we would have to put up with the hardship and do the best we could. Walking into the living room there was a fireplace that hopefully would help heat the house later in the fall and winter. No carpet on the floor or linoleum yet. Not a curtain on a window but that would change soon. I thought this old house will not be as nice as the farmhouse, that's for sure. We walked out the back door and looked up. On the ceiling of the porch in every corner were wasps and mud masons. They were swarming all around watching all the action. When they landed on us we would swat them away quickly before they could sting us. It was a job knocking all the nests down but it was our home now even though they were here first. Looking down at the end of the yard we saw for the first time the outhouse dad had built the week before. A toilet with two holes so my sister and I could visit together. Toilet paper was the Sears Roebuck catalogue. I was glad it did not have the slick colored pages yet. Later we could use it as our private hide away and gossip. It had a peep hole in the door for

144

light. No one could surprise us because we could see out. The floor was good and solid and in better shape then the house. In the bedroom we had a chamber pot so we didn't have to go out at night.

Our source of water was the spring over the hill. Two big buckets a day were carried to the house. Right after supper when we were through, dad said, " I want to talk to you two girls. Next time before you sit down to the table put the water on to heat. It will be hot when you finish then you can wash the dishes right away after clearing the table." We listened to him and made a habit of it and we had a lot more time in the evening. When we were washing dad's favorite coffee cup we accidentally broke it. He yelled from the other room, "Did you girls break something in there? Was it my coffee cup?" We were scared of the consequences so we lied and said, "No dad." We knew the truth would come out as early as the next morning. When evening came and it was time to retire to my bedroom for the first night I remember thinking. What a good feeling to have a home of our own. My father, brother, sister and I were altogether again and I was thrilled. That day started a new and different life for us siblings. We assumed responsibility for ourselves. During the night I dreamed my mother would be there in the morning and have breakfast ready for her family. It was just wishful thinking but what a wonderful dream.

The next morning dad spoke up after looking for his coffee cup, "Where is my favorite coffee cup?" I answered, "We broke it last night accidentally.""

He asked, Why did you lie to me?" " Well dad, I said a little too loud, you always throw such a fit when anything goes wrong. We didn't want to listen to a lecture. Now I want to tell you something. I want you to tell your mother we need some cups, cereal bowels, and some extra dishes. She has every cupboard filled and over flowing with dishes. I am sure she would be happy to send us some. We can''t keep house and cook without dishes and cooking pans." He looked up with surprise and said, "You sure are getting sassy!" I replied, "It's about time!" I was sixteen and starting to get an opinion about the way things were going to be. Francie and I assumed all the responsibility for the housekeeping and some chores that was not ours. Dad then made a special trip over to grandma's house. He returned with a big box of kitchen supplies, a few bars of lye soap and some window curtains. We wrote him a thank you note.

After a few days, there seemed to be something so familiar about the old house. My memories of the past were coming alive. The bent over tree in the back yard stirred up my thoughts about my childhood. Francie and I found the picture album that we treasured. It was kept safe in a box upstairs. There was a photo of this very same house with the slightly bent over tree. Another was of Aunt Pearl with my two little cousins. Also in the photo was my mother, brother, baby sister and I. Suddenly it came back to me, it was the day we visited when mother's sister lived here a long time ago.

Dad left us at home when he went to the store for groceries. He expected us to have all our chores finished when he returned. He couldn't drive the model T any longer it had given out. It had been a good car that took us many places these past several years. Memories of traveling with mom was one of the special things I loved about it. Dad's brother from Akron drove a Dodge touring car to West Virginia and gave it to him. That morning he started driving down our hill in the new car. Francie and I started right away and had our jobs done in a short time. Lazy bones Ronald went out on the porch to rest. In about a hour we heard the car coming a mile

146

down the road. It was noisy coming around the bend belching and sputtering. My brother jumped up. He would get a hard switching if he didn't have his chores done when dad came back. We knew this and felt sorry for him, as usual. Ronald started yelling for us to help him because dad would be good and mad if he hadn't done his jobs. We three had just finished when dad pulled up to the house. He looked things over and was pleased. My lazy brother was grinning ear to ear and took all the credit. If it hadn't been for that loud old car he would not have gotten by with that trick. We never tattled on him because we loved him.

What an ornery brother we had. He would hide behind the wood pile and watch for sister and I to wander towards the outhouse. He threw corn cobs at us and was a good shot, unfortunately for us. It made a big red spot on us where ever it hit. The outhouse was not fastened down. When we were inside he would come down and shake it, scaring us until we screamed. He never did any of these mischievous things when dad was home. We were on the look out for him every day.

In the summer Ronald and our cousin had left for a short adventure. A lot of the older boys in the country did the same thing. Riding the rails with characters such as bums and thieves. Landing in jail was a chance they took. They would sneak on a train by hiding in the box cars. It was an exciting way to see other parts of the country and my brother was itching to take off again. Dad had worried about him the whole time because it was extremely dangerous. One evening after supper Ronald started a conversation about school. He had quit in the middle of last year. He told dad if he would keep my sister and I home this school year he would not leave. Dad agreed. We did not have anyone to take up for us. We had to abide with dad's authority over us. Our district had not been notified that we had returned from Ohio. If they had known it would have been a different story. Sadly, we did what we were told. Ronald did not like school and discipline. He did not care about our welfare and I think a little jealous because we loved school. Missing those semesters caused us to graduate one year late. It was a miserable time in our lives. We missed school and our friends. There was only one good result. We passed our time reading the Bible story book given to us years ago by Aunt Ada over and over again. We felt like we were forgotten by everyone. I thought many times, if only mother was here!

October was a beautiful month at the homestead. It was totally different then at the other farm. More beautiful color in all the trees close to the house. Viewing wild animals out the windows. It was quite secluded and lonely.

Chilly November had snuck in and it was time for turkey shoots. Only men and older boys could participate. Dad and Ronald could not wait until Saturday. Their chores were finished by noon. Dad slung his one shot muzzle rifle over his shoulder as they took off down the road. Both of them were excellent shots so they were hard to beat in competition. Every participate paid a quarter a shot. All the money was put in the pot to pay for the prizes they could win which was mostly food. Flour, sugar, dry beans and flaked hominy. Each one had a sack to hopefully carry their winnings back home. Of course the grand prize was a big fat turkey. Ronald won the prize twice in a row and the turkey. When we saw them coming up the road that afternoon we were so excited. Dad was carrying a big sack and my brother a turkey over his back. Our first Thanksgiving dinner at the homestead was a plentiful array of food. We rarely missed visiting grandma and the family on Thanksgiving so dessert was at her farmhouse. Apple, peach, cherry, rhubarb and homemade ice cream! What a treat!

It was Christmas season. Dad was always sad this time of year. I understood, because this holiday brought back vivid memories of mom. We tried to bring some joy in his life especially during the week before Christmas. We certainly had a choice of trees. Pine trees covered the acreage. Large and small, with beautiful full branches covered with snow. We choose one that was perfect to decorate. Ronald cut in down then nailed it to a stand. It was just the right size. We would have to use our imagination because we did not have any decorations. Francie thought of our colored construction paper. We cut it in strips but did not have glue to make chains. Nothing was going to stop us now. Flour and water made the best glue and it worked like magic. Our brother was outside so it was safe to pop popcorn. We made our chains quickly and put them on the tree or he would have devoured it all in a minute. It was a different story when we made our cranberry chains. That was one fruit he wouldn't eat, thank goodness was our thoughts.

Red, green, yellow paper chains, red cranberry and white popcorn chains made a beautiful decorated tree. The only thing missing was lights. To our surprise the branches were strong enough to hold candles. Dad warned us about the danger of fire so, no candles. To give light to our creation we placed a lantern under it at night. That gave a wonderful glow to the whole room.

Every one in the community attended the Christmas program at church. I was already seated when dad came in and sat beside me. He was a bit tipsy I think. I leaned forward on the bench to hear the children say their pieces better. He pulled me back in my seat and loudly said, "Lean back here by your dad and be proud of him." I said, " I am proud of you dad, now lets enjoy the program." Everyone in the church laughed. We sat closer and more quiet then. Always an enjoyable program especially for the children.

Grandmother Null had brought our gifts that night. When we went home we opened them. Francie and I had identical dresses. I liked my blue dress with a red tie. When my sister opened hers she did not like it one bit. She took her gift upstairs and threw it in the corner. She said, "Our cousins wore their beautiful new dresses to the program and we get these plain dresses! It is not good enough for me. We are all four her grand daughters and I expect the same exact gifts for us." She was fourteen, very hurt and angry. I did not tell anyone especially grandma what she said and she never wore that dress. It was a difficult time of the year for everyone in the family. The only thing that allowed me to endure the season was those precious memories of mother. It seemed like yesterday to me when they floated through my mind that night.

The long winter months did not pass quickly as they did in previous years. Francie and I should have been in high school like other girls our age. We had no choice but to do what dad wanted, but it was not our decision. One thing I did look forward to was Saturday evenings. Most of the time we would visit the Null grandparents home. It was closer now to the homestead so it didn't take much time to drive there. Dad and Uncle Tom would play checkers for most of the evening. I didn't understand why they would sit for such a long time before making a move. We didn't care because all four of us girls would listen to Lum and Abner on the radio. We did not have a radio at home or at grandma's so it was fun and exciting to hear the latest news and programs.

I tolerated the winter. Early spring had sprung. I could not have made it through those months if it had not been for my sister. What a blessing she had always been to me. All the students in the community were celebrating the last day of school. Francie and I made it known to our family that we were positively not missing another year of high school. We were both scholars, besides we loved school and was determined this wasted school year would be the last.

We were allowed to start shopping for groceries and supplies. After all we were young ladies now and were running the household. Down by the river was Moat's Gristmill on the river bank. We could walk down the steep hill and be there in a jiffy. The local mill is where everyone had their flour and corn ground. Cornmeal was a staple. It was one of our favorites. Nothing better then beans and homemade butter on cornbread with chopped onion from the garden on top. On the first floor Ezra had a supply of utensils all kinds of pots, pans and crocks for sale. The women had a lot of choices. One of the latest items geared for women were feed sacks with a print on them. The grain companies had the bright idea of printing colorful flowers, animals and stripes on the bags. That was quite an enticement for the ladies to shop and not be left at home. They made dresses for their girls and shirts for the boys from the emptied bags. It was economical and fun for them to match up the patterns. Women were just starting to gain some freedom. It was the beginning of the joy of shopping without their husbands. In the past the men would do it for them. Products such as sugar, hominy, oats and coffee just to name a few were on the long shelves. All the kids loved the buckets full of many kinds of candy. My favorite was the stick candy. The best flavors were cinnamon, root beer, teaberry and chocolate. I could make a stick last a long time by breaking it in small pieces. When dad would go, he always bought a few haystack chocolates and shared them with us. I took a brown feed sack to carry our goods home. We didn't have big baskets like some of the women, it was all we had. I often thought we would have had a better life if mom was here. My dad always said, "never the less," meaning things could not be changed. So, never the less, I still missed my mother but that did not change things. I loved and respected my father dearly. No one would dare say anything against him to me or they would have been in trouble.

It was a warm day so all three of us were resting at the end of the bed in the living room. We had nothing to do so we were bored. Uncle Tom surprised us when he knocked at the door. He had stopped by to pay Ronald for a job he had done for him at the Null farm. He then asked my brother if he wanted to stroll down to the river and fish for awhile. I know he was disappointed when Ronald said, "No it's too darn hot." So my uncle replied he might as well go anyways. We continued resting when suddenly Ronald jumped up and yelled, "Where is my money, one of you girls took it and where are you hiding it?" My sister and I were dumb founded. We assured him we didn't take it or know where it was. Looking in his pockets, yelling like a bani rooster, showing off as usual. In a while he walked over to the bed and pulled out something from under the blanket. " Gee Wiz I thought for sure you girls had taken my money!" he said with a grin on his face. We had to put up with some kind of foolishness from him every time dad would leave. He was always looking for trouble. If he could devil us in any way or embarrass us, he was in his glory.

Girls in the country did not have very much of an opportunity to do exciting things together. When we heard about our girlfriend Cora, trying to find a place for a few of the neighborhood girls to go camping, we were excited. She asked her brother to check around. He contacted a local person that knew of a spot for about twelve girls. We could go the next weekend and it was close to a lake, perfect.

Activities and swimming were going to be fun. Dad agreed for us to go. Now we would have to gather the supplies we needed. Aunt Belle helped us get the clothes and food we were supposed to take. Grandma and her were always so nice to us and supportive. A neighbor volunteered to drive all of us and our supplies in his truck.

Two adults went with us to help put up the tent. That was a good idea because we could not have assembled that big tent up by ourselves. First we marked our place to sleep. Of course my sister and I quickly laid our blankets side by side. It was a beautiful day and we were anxious to head for the lake. On that hot summer day it would feel good because the water was cool. My sis did not go in the lake but I liked it. Cora was the director and in charge. When she said it was time to bunk down that"s what we did. Our first night was dark and scary. Some of the girls didn't get much sleep because of the barking dogs, including me.

Morning finally arrived and all of us were confused about breakfast. We figured out we had to make due with the cornflakes we brought. We choose partners for the three days we were going to be there. I chose a girl my age named Tammy. She was real pretty with long brown hair. After breakfast the water looked inviting, so away we went down to the lake. We went in swimming and was splashing around and having a good time. Right then we heard a commotion down stream. Of course we were curious and wanted to find the source of the noise. There was a house boat with four boys that were living there for the summer. They invited us on board. Father had cautioned me to be very slow to get acquainted with strange boys. We heeded his advise and returned to camp. When we reached the camp, a lot more teenagers had arrived. I noticed a nice looking boy, named Kenny. He liked me so we started going swimming together. He wanted my sister and I to meet his mother. He lived close by so we walked to his house and met his mother. She was real nice. Her cat had a litter of kittens she wanted to give to a good home. We couldn't resist and picked out two we wanted. She agreed for us to get them right before leaving. We were hungry so she served us sandwiches and milk. We thanked her and told her we would see her the next day. A small store was near by so we bought a few groceries for one more day. It was a nice experience but the next morning we were ready to go home. We never knew what caused my sister to become very ill and weak. She wasn't feeling well but we had to hurry up anyways. We rushed to pick up the kittens before the truck would leave. We just made it in time for our trip back home. There was no one there to greet us or help us carry our supplies. We left them with our cousin Sally. She was one of the neighbor girls that also went. We then climbed into the john boat and crossed the river. Then up the bank towards the house. We were carrying the kittens up the steep hill, we couldn't leave them behind. We stopped because Francie had to lay down and rest. I was worried, she was getting weaker and looked really sick. When dad came home I rushed to tell him she was ill. He thought she may have eaten some food that was spoiled. After giving her a big glass of cold milk he told her to go to bed early and rest all night. I showed him our cute little kittens. He thought for just a minute then said we could keep them. The next morning Francie was much better. Here came a visitor, it was Cora the camp leader. She had heard about my sister becoming ill and was anxious to check on her. Relieved when she saw my sister was well.

154

She was so glad no one was hurt on the camping trip. Cora seemed to be sincerely concerned. One of her brothers was a smite. He repaired mostly broken wagon wheels. Those West Virginia roads were rough and rocky. He would always say when anyone brought him something to repair, "By thunder I can fix anything!" and he could. The whole family was ready to assist friend and neighbors whatever the problem might be. Most country folk were willing to help each other that's just the way it had always been.

In a few days we decided to give our pets a name. After giving it a lot of thought, Francie named hers after her best friend Caroline. I liked the movie Zorro, so my black kitten was named after my hero. One afternoon when I was playing with Zorro outside, we had a visitor. He had a noisy, old beat up car. When he had to give it a lot of gas to make it up the hill, it sounded like a thunder bolt. Well, it scared my kitten. He ran up my bare leg and hung on for dear life with his toenails. It didn't take long for me to heist up my dress and gently pull him loose. The scratches hurt for awhile but that was O.K. I understood he was trying to find a place to hide. I took him inside until the boy left. That was the only time I can remember being unhappy to see a visitor.

I always wondered why my sister had such a beloved way with all animals. I found out the answer from grandmother Null. She told me something that revealed the truth. I did not know when my mother Ella was a child she had eight kittens and cats. When her dad went to the barn to milk, mom and her cats followed him every time. She had several bowls to feed them milk. After milking her dad filled a bucket up with fresh milk. Then she would carefully fill each bowl over flowing for her cats. Her pets stayed in the barn at night. Early every morning they would greet her on the back porch. This was a lovely story about my mom, told to me by her mother. Cats were one of my sister's favorite pets so I knew it was true, like mother, like daughter.

The hot summer months were the only time the river was warm enough to swim. We would get in the john boat and row over to the sand bar in the middle of the river. It was quite shallow and we were not afraid. The deep part we left to our cousins that swam like ducks. They would dive under the water and never once thought of any danger.

All of us had wonderful times together laughing and happy as we could be. Cats didn't like the water and they could not swim. We penned Caroline and Zorro up because we knew they would have followed us.

Francie and I planted our first garden. We had green beans, our favorite vegetable. We had fresh lettuce we had planted in February for our summer salads. Tomatoes were ripening and we were anxious to pick a few. Our own recipe was to cream them on the stove with a little sugar. We poured that over biscuits left over from breakfast or homemade bread. Lots of fresh churned butter. What a delicious meal that made. We had become pretty good cooks despite not having a mother to teach us.

My sister noticed Caroline was getting real rolly poly and that meant only one thing. We never knew who the father of the litter was but we didn't care. She came to the door one morning. Francie fed her and knew she had her kittens the night before. She hid them for a while but we finally found them. We sat quietly in the barn knowing she would lead us to them if we waited long enough. Soon we spied Caroline leaping up to the loft. Up the ladder we scurried. There they were, four kittens. Two female with tiger stripes and two jet black males. They were adorable. We put a basket with a blanket in it and put it in the feedbox. We placed the kittens gently in there. The mother cat climbed right in and started nursing. Zorro kept his distance for a long time. Male cats knew better then to get close to new born kittens. He slowly eased his way back in. Finally he was part of the family pets again.

Ronald had cut down a tree in the woods. Two baby squirrels fell out of the nest. He took them to Caroline to nurse. In about two days she brought one of the baby squirrels to the house. It had been smothered accidentally by the bigger kittens. I guessed she didn't know the difference between her kittens and the baby squirrels. When she laid it on the porch she cried and cried. I thought there was a lot we did not know about animals and how they grieve. This was an unusual happening but it is true. When the kittens were old enough to be away from Caroline they played in the branches of the old Catawba tree. We watched them for hours running and trying to catch each other. That was one of our greatest joys of the summer of 1935.

It was late summer and not much to do after we had our chores done. It was hot as the dickens so we went out on the porch and slipped off our dresses. All that we had on was under clothes. It didn't make any difference. We hardly ever had any company, especially in the middle of the day. The cool breeze felt good on our hot bodies. I rubbed Ponds cold cream on Francie's back. Both of us were fair skinned so we could not sun bathe very long before burning. I thought she looked beautiful just like a movie star stretched out on the lounge. About that time a man came around the corner of the house. He stepped up on the porch without looking. We were so frightened and embarrassed we nearly fainted. He was as surprised as we were because he turned his back. We slipped our dresses on quickly. I asked, " Who are you, and what are you doing here?" He answered, " I'm a friend of Coon Lewis. My name is Frank and one of the neighbors said I could buy whiskey here." "The neighbors are badly mistaken. My sister and I live here with our dad. I would like to know who told you such a lie. I am angry and will certainly tell my dad as soon as he gets home. Now turn around and leave the way you came!" I ordered. He turned around and said, " I am so sorry I frightened you two beautiful girls. Tell your father I think you two resemble your lovely mother. I knew her many years ago you know." He tipped his hat and headed down the hill. We told dad about the stranger but not all the details. Our father's nickname was Coon. We were told he was the youngest lad in the country to hunt raccoon. That's the name he was called by most of the time, even by his sisters. After that startling episode Francie decided we would have to find a look out spot. She didn't want another surprise from a stranger. In the front of the house there was an old tree that had fallen in a storm. We found a safe place to sit among the limbs. From that view point we could see in all directions. It was a great lookout.

My sister wrote letters and would read. She had beautiful script. Our cousins were thrilled to receive a letter from her.

I liked to read Bible stories and write poems. We felt safe and happy in our hideout. I thought many times that we would at least have these wonderful memories. Those many hours that we spent in that old tree seemed to make our lonely days better. I still missed my mother and pondered about what the stranger had said. Everyone that mentioned her name always had kind comments and told me how special she was.

Summer was coming to an end and everyone knew we were definitely starting back to high school in September. No question about it!

Chapter Eight
Cario High School

MY SISTER AND I DIDN'T GET MUCH sleep the night before school started. I dreamed of not getting up in time and missing the bus. It was a long night. We were up at 6 am so we thought we had plenty of time. It was quite a long ways for us to walk to get to the bus stop. Down the hill, crossing the river in the boat then walking through the field to the bus stop for the high school students on the other side of the road. We saw that the bus driver was waiting for us when we finally arrived out of breath. It was a very exciting time at Cairo High school that day for my sister and I. We were so thrilled to have the privilege of attending this year. When we came home that evening and every other one, there were our chores to do. I had to cook supper on that old dilapidated stove. My sister had to feed the chickens and gather eggs. We were always ready for bed early during the week.

I was especially fond of my English teacher. Maybe one reason we bonded was because she had red hair like mine! Her name was Miss Robey. She liked me, I always listened closely to everything she said. I think this is why I had an idea about what questions were going to be on the next test. Taking a lot of notes during class helped also. She asked me to correct test papers at home. I thought I was special for her to trust me. Some of the boys would attach notes to their test papers but I never answered them. I felt almost like a teacher! The whole class had to take a semester exam, and of course I did well.

I think grading papers helped me better understand our subjects, especially English.

Occasionally there were special events at various locations. My sister and I heard about a box supper being held at the Petroleum school. It was not too far away and we really wanted to go. The ladies were to have enough food for a small meal for two people. Mostly sandwiches and a slice of pie or cake. It was an auction and the men or boys had to bid for a particular box. They knew which girl had brought which box so the bidding could get quite exciting if the girl was popular. It always was a lot of fun when they had one at our little country school. We attended but never had been old enough to participate. When we asked dad if we could go he said no. After decorating two boxes with pretty tissue paper and aqua tensile we thought he would change his mind. We were all ready to leave but he refused to let us go with him. Our hearts were broken and we both cried. We were unhappy with him for a few days. I thought he was an over protective father or the reasons was unknown to me why he didn't allow us to go. We missed the box supper and was very disappointed.

It was October and extremely cold. There was a thin layer of ice on the river. Francie was ahead of me carrying our school books. I heard her scream for me in the distance. When I came closer to the boat landing I saw her. She had slipped clear down the bank and was standing up to her knees in water but holding the books above her head. She was looking angry at me, and said, "You better get down here right away and paddle the boat to me real slow. Where have you been anyways?" I knew I was in deep trouble. She put the books on the seat of the boat and walked in the water to the shore holding onto the side. She had a hard time climbing back up that icy bank. We proceeded to cross to the other shore. Some of our cousins helped her to get to their house near by. She dried out in front of the gas stove, and changed into some clean clothes as fast as she could. We heard the bus coming, then it came to a stop. One of the smart acting boys asked her why she had went swimming so early in the morning. He asked her if she didn't know the water was wet that day. All the boys had a big laugh. If it hadn't been for her good friend and cousin, Evelyn Doris she would have missed a day of school. That would have been unfortunate because she and I had perfect attendance.

Dad looked the situation over after that incident. I guess he decided it was a dangerous situation especially in the winter. He built a ramp so we did not have to go down the bank to get into the boat from then on. We did have more company now that family and friends could get there more safely.

That Sunday at church we truly counted our blessings. We were thankful everyone in our family made it through the last week without any problems. I was silently thinking about my sister's accident and thanked Jesus for his watch care over her.

The bus ride to school was beautiful on winter mornings. On the route the bus was unloaded before crossing over the river. The bus driver drove slowly on the covered bridge. All of us students had to follow on foot. The bridge was not safe with the weight of the bus and kids together. It was dark inside but I could see the light at the end of the bridge. There were no exceptions, we had to do this two times every school day. We then loaded back on and continued until we reached the small town of Cairo. The driver stopped in front of the drug store for us to unload. We all trudged over to the railroad tunnel, crossed the road and walked up the hill. At the bottom was the100 steps we would again have to climb to reach the high school. I always loved going up to the top floor looking out the windows at the small friendly town below. My junior year went fast. During the rest period I concentrated on my studies using other students books. The next days homework needed to be completed before I left school. While others had stars in their eyes, my mind was always about making good grades to make the honor roll.

School activities were held in the evenings most of the time. Not a basketball or football game did we ever attend. Once Francie and I left school for the day we were never able to return that night. It was too far, no transportation and too many chores. February 28, 1936 was my eighteenth birthday. The day passed as fast as it came. I didn't have very many clothes or dresses to wear that year. At least I was able to get an education like the other students despite my wardrobe. My mind often drifted on that long ride back home from school. I knew if mom was here she would have made my sister and I lovely dresses that would have out shined all the rest. There would have been parties for our friends and we would have never missed any social events. I missed her. The last semester was ending and spring in the country had arrived. Summer vacation would begin soon.

Now I had to wait until September to start my senior year.

I was going to try to make the summer go fast by keeping busy. My Aunt Grace was one of my favorites relatives, married to our ornery Uncle Tom. She was an angel with three children. My cousins, Pauline the oldest, serious and pretty, red headed Mary Lee loving and very special. Then there was Kitty, cute as a button and a charmer like her dad. She knew she could get her way with everyone. She certainly did, she was the baby of the family.

That summer my aunt asked if I could do some work for her. I was glad to oblige. One afternoon I ironed twenty six outfits for Kitty. Her mother dressed all three of her girls in pretty clothes. Kitty would change anytime she had a spot on a dress so there was a lot more for me to iron. I loved visiting with that side of the family. I always thought of my mother when I was there.

One of my jobs was to prepare supper for the hired hands. Dad was helping that day cutting hay. Meals were composed of mostly garden vegetables that time of the year. Big heads of cabbage was one of the yields. I added some ham to the pot and that was the entree. I baked biscuits in their modern oven. I thought, I sure wish we had an oven like this so we could bake biscuits. I placed the large pot of cabbage on the table. All the men ate hardily. Uncle Tom was late coming home from the oil fields that day. I noticed he didn't have much of an appetite. When I asked what was wrong he told me to look in the pot. There were two big cabbage worms floating on top. I told him there was nothing wrong with a little extra meat beside the ham to make a good dish of cabbage. He didn't think that was funny. I was told later he never ate a meal without looking it over real good before taking a bite. When dad and I returned home that evening I asked him how he liked my biscuits. He said, " I am sure tired of pancakes grilled on top of our old stove. Biscuits like you made would taste mighty good to me with our meals!" Next day he drove over to the local hardware store and bought a stove pipe oven. It actually hooked up to the existing pipe. It took a long time to produce enough heat to bake. Guess you know what we baked for supper that very same evening! The only thing the ancient coal and wood stove was good for was heating the kitchen. I asked myself, why did dad wait so long to get us an oven?

Chapter Nine
Independence Day 1936

WE KNEW SUMMER HAD OFFICIALLY ARRIVED when the men started talking about the up coming baseball competition. Teams had been formed. In the country the most important event was the rival ball games. They were always played on Saturday. The team members were mostly young men that were very competitive and good players. My sister and I were quite excited because the Petroleum team was scheduled to play our local boys consisting of many we already knew. I thought maybe we would meet a few new guys! The game was to be played at the Rusk ball field. It was located right below our house so we could walk straight over the hill and be there in a minute. We rushed down to the field because we didn't want to miss anything. It was the fourth of July, Independence day 1936, a beautiful sunny day, perfect weather for the game. That celebration was to became one of the most important days of my life. We watched as old cars, trucks and anything on wheels came slowly up the hill. A Dodge coupe with a rumble seat immediately caught my eye. I watched as a tall handsome young man climbed out of the drivers side. Then a good looking blonde guy joined him. I thought it sure would be fun to get acquainted with them.

Dad was already on the side line. He thought he could make some money by selling lemon aid and sweet tea to those thirsty players, and of course everyone else who came. The sweeter the tea, the more they would buy, was his refrain. He had made a ten gallon crock of tea that morning. Not as much lemonade because it was not liked as well as tea. Aunt Belle was there with a cigar box to hold all the proceeds. She was in charge of the money and making change. The crowd started to gather and the ball game was about to begin. The teams had taken their place and the first ball was pitched. All of a sudden it began to sprinkle. The boys were worried. If it stormed they would not be able to drive their vehicles down the wet muddy road. They would be stuck on the hill. Before we knew it rain came down in buckets, it was a cloud burst. Some of the team scurried to their cars and left as quick as they could. Those two fellows in the Dodge opened their car doors and offered for Francie and I to get out of the heavy down pour. We exchanged names and that was about all before the storm subsided. Too bad for my father and aunt because the tent and all the drinks were ruined. The cigar box was knocked over and most of the money blew away.

After we climbed out of the car, one of the players yelled, "Lets Play ball!" They were short of players so I volunteered to be the pitcher. The tall handsome guy was the umpire. Every ball I threw he called it a strike.

The catcher became angry and threw me a real hard ball that went through my glove. It hit me in the eye and knocked me down flat on the ground. The good looking umpire picked me up and held on to me until I got my bearings. The young man with him was in an argument with a fellow from our team. I found out then they were brothers. The umpire settled him down and he left with us after making friends with my cousin. They offered to drive my sister and I back to our house. I thought, this must be my lucky day! The umpire's name was Mayford and his brother was Lou. The handsome tall

166

one had just returned from C.C.C. camp in Elkins, West Virginia. This government program was called the Civilian Conservation Corp. It was established for unmarried young men to earn money in hard times. They built roads, lodges and many other projects that would benefit the future generations. I was impressed. He asked if we wanted to meet the next afternoon. I told them to meet us at the Methodist church. I couldn't wait for Sunday!

The next morning Francie and I went to the Baptist Sunday school class but didn't stay for church. Dad had dinner ready. We hurriedly washed dishes. We informed dad we were going to Aunt Belles church. He had no idea there would be two boys there we just met. We hurried down the hill to cross the river. I guess I was in too big a hurry because I tore my dress on a scrub thorn tree.

My sister pinned it together with one of the thorns, and we were on our way again. We ran across the mill dam, under the mill and came up on the other side of the road. The guys were parked at the gristmill instead of at the church. Mayford had brought a friend for my sister. I think Lou already was interested in a girl he had called Belle. My friend had a pair of dark sunglasses. I never had a pair so I wanted to try them on. We couldn't stay too long so it was a short visit. They asked us if we wanted to meet them at the Baptist church evening service. Of course, we agreed but held on to the sunglasses as a little insurance they would be there. That night they took us home in the Dodge.

The next Saturday was another baseball game. Ronald and Bob were going. To our surprise they asked my sister and I if we wanted to go with them. The game was going to be at Petroleum. We saw some of our cousins and friends in the crowd. I was looking diligently until I spotted that 6 foot handsome young man I had met last week. I knew he was as happy to see me as I was him. After the game I told him where I was going to be working that week in town. He dropped by and asked me for a date. When he picked me up I introduced him to my father. He liked my new friend right away. We started dating steady after that. We would take Francie and her girlfriend quite often with us. Everyone liked Mayford and I did too! That summer was the first year I can say was fun and exciting. It passed quickly because I now had some one in my life I adored.

My senior year was approaching. I was looking forward to my last year in high school. It was different now. I had goals for my future and knew I would achieve them. I was determined to make the honor role again as in the past.

Latin for the second time was important. This subject was necessary for a nursing career. That was what I was striving for at that time.

Our sponsor for the class was Miss Wilson. I liked her immediately. All the boys paid attention to her because she was single and pretty. She made arrangements for all special events for our class. After a few weeks she scheduled a banquet in the early evening that we all attended. It gave us an opportunity to become acquainted with our classmates. During school hours it was difficult to get to know other students. I thought this was a clever idea and we all admired her because she truly cared for us.

Another teacher asked me to grade papers at home for him. He said he did not have enough time. When he told me the school system would pay me six dollars a month I excepted right away. Many nights it was midnight before I went to bed. Grading papers was time consuming. It was part of my job to give the student the final grade. I assumed the teacher trusted me. He just glanced at the papers when I turned them over to him and said thanks.

One particular morning turned into a unusual school day. My cousin Sally asked me if I wanted to skip school and visit with Madeline Morrison. She said her mother had passed away and she had to quit school. Another thing I was not aware of was that her home had burned down and the family moved to an apartment in Cairo. Of course I was devastated and knew how she felt losing her mother. My mind was made up quickly and I thought it was the right thing to do. Madeline was glad to see us and we helped her catch up on a lot of house work she couldn't get done by herself. We tried to cheer her up and the time passed fast. Before we realized it was almost three o'clock. We said good by and wished her luck. I ran most of the way to school to get my books and coat. Mr. Ramsey, the principal held the door open for me. He never said a word as I streaked by him. I think he knew we were just trying to do a good deed because he never called us to his office the next day. That was the only day I skipped school. I rushed down the long flight of steps and over to town where the bus driver had the motor running. The kids had there heads out the windows yelling, "Come on bucket, you can make it!" As I jumped on the bus the driver said he would not have left me and I was glad of that. Everyone clapped and cheered while we pulled away. Down the road we went. My nickname was Bucket. Once a week I would bring a bucket of eggs to the store for a few groceries. Bartering was a common practice in those days and everyone benefitted.

My steady boyfriend and I didn't have many times we could see each other during the winter months. The roads were snow covered most days and dangerous to travel.

The Romine family had a lumber mill. All the boys worked hard cutting trees in the forest. They then pulled the logs by mules to the mill so the logs could be cut into lumber. Much of the lumber was then loaded onto a train headed for Harrisville to sell. Mayford was one of the oldest of four brothers that worked for their dad. He had a lot of responsibility and not much time. On occasion we would meet at the Sunday evening church service. At that time we would plan our next date. I was not interested in anyone else and he only had eyes for me. The boys at school could not compete with Mayford.

Winter of 1937 was exceptionally snowy and cold. Our family made it over to Grandma Lewis's for Thanksgiving. It took a lot longer than usual to drive because of the condition of the snow covered roads. No snow plows, only shovels and determination to enjoy a rare holiday occasion we were not going to miss. All of the families traveled long distances to be together this year. There was quite a large group. Most of the grandchildren were adults by this time. I enjoyed visiting with my younger cousin Jenny Rose who I hadn't seen for awhile. It was almost like a Lewis family reunion.

Christmas arrived so quickly. This holiday came and went without anything unusual happening. Church, family and snow were the daily routine. As always I missed mother in a special way every Christmas. Although this year it seemed to be a little bit different. I had someone in my life who filled my thoughts and was much happier than ever before. Because of the severe weather Mayford and I were unable to see each other during the holidays.

Time passed and I was back in school looking forward to spring. Finally graduation was almost here. It would be the last chance to see and talk to our fellow

170

classmates for a long time. The end of the year play was an evening never to be forgotten. I played the part of a man. The play ended with a great round of applause.

Cousins, Rhoda and Monelle had talked Francie and I into taking a ride with four boys. They were from my class. After the play, all eight of us climbed into a Model A Ford. It was a tight squeeze but we thought this was going to be fun. I thought we were traveling down that steep hill too fast. It was dangerous for an experienced driver, let alone our young driver Olan. He yelled out, " something is wrong with the brakes and I can't slow her down!" I knew we were in real trouble. The further he drove the faster the car went. Quick thinking, Olan saw a side road and made a fast turn to keep us from crashing. The old Ford jeered to the left and flipped over in a ditch. We all screamed like the end was near! To make it worse we couldn't get the doors open. A crowd of people gathered after seeing the accident. It took a few minutes, that seemed like hours but some men pried the doors open. I was the last one to come out. I felt my under pants slipping down. I gripped them tightly. A young man finally pulled me out with my pants still in tact. I had a secret, Thank God no one discovered. I had worn my brother's underwear that night for the part of playing a policeman. Why? I'll never know. With a lot of help the men turned the car right side up. Everyone had to find a way home. Fortunately, we were lucky. Dad had attended the performance. He had insisted on escorting my sister and I that evening. That was an exception to the rule and we were glad he came. It could have been a sad night for eight families of the class of 1937 and bitter memories. God had to be watching over us that evening. We had another chance to live wonderful and full lives.

Graduation from Cairo High School was a gratifying   accomplishment for the fifty one seniors. An end to wonderful days spent studying and all the other activities associated with high school. Now I was definitely ready to pursue my future. I knew I would miss the companionship with my fellow students. These thoughts probably go through the minds of everyone who loved school. My dad, brother and sister attended. Way in the back I spied a young man that looked familiar. It was Mayford! I was thrilled that he cared enough to celebrate with my family and I. It would have been a perfect day if my mother could have been there. I knew she would have been proud of her honor student.

I was anxious to continue my quest to become a nurse. Dr. Douglas knew of my desire and contacted me. He took me to St. Joseph's hospital at Parkersburg, West Virginia.

This was the largest town close to where we lived. He arranged an interview with the Sister of nurses. I thought she was pleased with my enthusiasm. She offered me a uniform to put on and wanted me to start training that very same say. I declined because I felt I should talk it over with my father before accepting the position. He was totally against me working for that particular hospital.

My Aunt Ellen knew I was looking for a job. She thought of a couple who would need a housekeeper soon. I went back in town the next day. The people she had referred me to were Mr. and Mrs. Andrews. I found out it would be not only keeping house but taking care of the lady of house who was bedridden. I needed a job so I accepted the position. They were a nice family and treated me well. The city streetcar ran right behind their home. I lost a few hours sleep but I finally became used to it.

It didn't take long before Mayford found out where I was working. He didn't waste any time coming to see me. We made plans to be together every Saturday evening. Movies was the entertainment we enjoyed each week. We both looked forward to watching the continued series of Zorro, my hero.

One week day evening after supper I was sitting on the front porch. All of a sudden a young man came up on the porch unannounced. He said, "Hi Marj!" I realized after a few seconds he was a brother of a friend. I was startled and asked, "How did you know where I was and why are you here?" He said on of the neighborhood boys told him and he thought he would pay me a visit. I told him I was not allowed to go anywhere during the week, the family needed me. Just then Mr. Andrews came out and said it would be fine if I wanted to have the evening off. Boy was I ever stuck between a rock and a hard place. I said I would go with him to the movie since he had came so far. I definitely did not want to go anywhere with him. Never the less, we jumped on the streetcar and left. When we were returning he offered to escort me back to the house. I told him to stay on the streetcar and to never come back, I was not interested in anyone but Mayford. I would find my way back just fine without him. The next Saturday Mayford admitted he knew all about it. I apologized and it was never mentioned again. I'm sure he knew I didn't care for anyone but him.

I only worked there a short time before dad came knocking at the Andrew's door. His brother from Akron, Ohio had called and needed one of the family to come and take care of my Aunt Maude. Uncle Dallas said she was very ill. Of course everyone thought I was the perfect candidate. I'm sure dad thought this would discourage me from wanting to become a nurse. Nonetheless, I was on my way to Akron and had no choice in the matter. I was so lonely and homesick especially leaving Mayford. We kept in touch by letters, I mean love letters! We couldn't stand the separation any longer. Mayford asked me to come home and marry him. I accepted immediately and left for West Virginia as soon as I could make the arrangements. My childhood had ended without a mother. When I was married in 1938, I started life as an adult. I looked forward to my future with the love of my life. Sweet memories of my Mother I knew would remain through out my days. Happiness with my husband overshadowed all the past sadness of Living Without A Mother.

www.ingramcontent.com/pod-product-compliance
Lightning Source LLC
Chambersburg PA
CBHW031301090426
42742CB00007B/552